# OPERATION GEORGE

A Gripping True Crime Story of an Audacious Undercover Sting

Mark Dickens with Stephen Bentley

Hendry Publishing Ltd

LONDON, ENGLAND

Abridged Large Print Editon

Copyright © 2022 by **Mark Dickens and Stephen Bentley**

All rights reserved. No part of this publication may be reproduced, distributed, or transmitted in any form or by any means, without prior written permission.

**Hendry Publishing Ltd**
**20-22 Wenlock Road**
**London, N1 7GU, United Kingdom**
www.hendrypublishing.com

Publisher's Note: This is a work of nonfiction. Some names have been changed, no characters invented, no events fabricated.

Book Cover Design: 100 Covers

**Operation George/ Mark Dickens and Stephen Bentley**
 -- 1st ed. Large Print

Large Print ed. ISBN 9781739813642

# CONTENTS

**The Targets** ............................................................. 1
   *When Julie Met George* ........................................ 5

**Genocide** ................................................................ 11

**Interview Room, Belfast** ............................. 15

**The Nelson Family Home** ............................. 19

**California Dreaming** ........................................ 24

**Colin Port** ............................................................. 33

**Down the Rabbit Hole** ..................................... 41

**Liz** .............................................................................. 50

**Exeter** ..................................................................... 69

**Cornwall** ................................................................. 85

**Lizzie** ....................................................................... 92
   *Dave S and Sam* .................................................. 96

**Neil** ........................................................................... 105

**First Meeting** ...................................................... 116

# Robbie a Fixture ... 121
# Slough ... 127
# Cash in Transit ... 131
# The Reversing Lorry ... 142
# Work of Art ... 158
# A Thousand Fags and Friction ... 178
# Torch the Trailer ... 188
# On the Piss in Plymouth ... 203
# Play Fighting ... 212
# Swinger ... 223
# Barbara Windsor ... 236
# Paranoia ... 245
## Police National Computer (PNC) ... 249
## Jimmy and the RUC Officer ... 259
# The Cutting Room Floor ... 267
## The Sherpa Hat ... 268
## PAG-IN-TON ... 273
## Lucky Robbie ... 275
## The Kebab Shop ... 281
## Roof Lining ... 285

**Missing Notebook** ...................................................... **289**

**The Voice** ..................................................................... **311**

**The Strike** ................................................................... **327**

**Interviews** ................................................................... **338**

**Bail** ............................................................................... **348**

**Belfast** ......................................................................... **353**

**The Admissions** ......................................................... **366**
   *Alcohol and Drugs* ................................................. *378*
   *Gibson Legal Issues* ............................................... *383*

**Sentencing and Appeal** ............................................. **396**
   *The Appeal of William James Fulton* ..................... *399*

**Unanswered Questions** ............................................. **404**
   *Who Killed Rosemary Nelson?* ............................... *404*
   *Who Pulled the Trigger?* ......................................... *409*
   *Historical Enquiries Team (HET)* ........................... *417*

# CHAPTER 1

## The Targets

The following true story is not about Rosemary Nelson, the Troubles *per se* nor Northern Ireland, although they feature out of necessity. We feel that from the outset it is worthwhile to set out a background to the events and locations of this book and a brief history of the Troubles in that part of Northern Ireland. Whilst this book tells the amazing story of possibly the most audacious undercover sting in the world, we also acknowledge the grief suffered by so many on both sides of the sectarian divide in that part of the United Kingdom. In writing this book, we can assure you we also felt the pain endured by so many innocent people.

William James Fulton and Muriel Gibson were from Portadown, a small town in County Armagh, Northern Ireland. Sadly, it is better known as the scene of the Drumcree conflict rather than the birthplace of notable people like Lady Mary Peters (Olympic athlete), Gloria Hunniford (TV personality) and Martin O' Neill (football manager). It is located about twenty-five miles southwest of Belfast. In the 1980s and 1990s its population was made up of about seventy percent Protestants and almost thirty percent Catholics. Garvaghy Road is in the middle of an area of housing that is largely populated by Catholics. Lurgan is a short drive away; about six miles separates it from Portadown. Lurgan was the location of Rosemary Nelson's law practice.

The Drumcree conflict is a dispute over the right of Protestants and loyalists to hold parades mainly to commemorate the so-called Glorious Revolution of 1688. The occasion is known by many as 'The Twelfth.' It was first held in the late 18th century in Ulster and it celebrates the victory of Protestant King William of Orange over Catholic King James II at the Battle of the Boyne in 1690, which began the Protestant Ascendancy in Ireland. Residents of Garvaghy Road and the surrounding Catholic district object to what they view as "triumphalist" Orange marches through their area. Rosemary Nelson, a Catholic solicitor, was the figurehead and spokesperson for the Garvaghy Road Residents' Coalition as well as representing the coalition in legal matters until she was assassinated on 15 March 1999. Sam Kinkaid, the RUC officer who played a leading role in the investigation of Rosemary Nelson's murder, described the area (Portadown) as "second only to North Belfast in terms of sectarianism.[1]" The sophisticated bomb device that blew up Rosemary Nelson's car and killed her is where our story begins. A loyalist paramilitary splinter group naming themselves the Red Hand Defenders claimed responsibility for the killing. At that time, William James Fulton and Muriel Landry née Gibson (referred to as Gibson throughout the remainder of this book) were members of the Loyalist Volunteer Force – the LVF. Soon after the bombing, Fulton fled to the United States and Gibson relocated to England. In this story of Operation George, all the names of the undercover police officers (UCOs) used are pseudonyms. Some are the same aliases as used in evidential transcripts and sanctioned

---

[1] Para 6.7 Nelson Inquiry. Full report can be accessed at https://www.gov.uk/government/publications/the-rosemary-nelson-inquiry-report

by the judge to preserve their anonymity whilst giving evidence at the trials of William James Fulton and Muriel Gibson at Belfast Crown Court. The names or nicknames of other UCOs and Cover Officers are fabricated aliases to protect their anonymity and thus prevent any kind of criminal retribution against them or their families. In the same vein, the authors are sparing in using details of any undercover officer such as physical descriptions, accents, backgrounds, and the like to preserve anonymity.

## When Julie Met George

Operation Julie and Operation George are light years away from each other in more ways than one. Undercover policing has drastically changed owing to modern 'UK Police PLC' attitudes and policies. The contrasts between 1970s Operation Julie and 21st Century

Operation George undercover policing are like night and day.

Perhaps now is an opportune moment to explain what is entailed to become a Level 1 UCO then to be entered into the national register. It's a world apart from the Operation Julie days when straight from being a member of a surveillance team, a detective would be asked by a boss if they wanted to go undercover. No training in those days. They made up a back story on the fly and then they were straight into the deep end. Sink or swim! For some time now, undercover officers are recruited and must attend a national training course. They are evaluated to see if they are suitable and are eventually set free to establish a legend and back story. Those are the two things they will fall back on and carry with them for the remainder of their undercover careers.

Essentially, it's a case of who they say they are and not who they really are. They will spend time in certain locations, establishing their faces by socialising and getting to be known in the area as Mr X or Mrs Y. That strengthens their credentials if someone checks them out. Occasionally, they may have to repeat that exercise if there is a good reason to change location. If an UCO has special skills, so much the better. For example, Robbie, one of the Operation George UCOs, appeared to have a licence to drive trucks, as it's known from the transcripts that he held himself out as a lorry driver in his dealings with Jim Fulton.

Unlike Bentley's pioneering undercover days, as described in his memoir Operation Julie[2], these Operation George officers belong to a modern era of covert policing. The story of

---

[2] Stephen Bentley, *Undercover: Operation Julie – The Inside Story,* Hendry Publishing, 2017 and *Operation Julie: The gripping inside story of Britain's biggest drug bust,* Ebury Spotlight, 2022

Operation George highlights the sophisticated methods deployed by modern law enforcement. Those methods and techniques are all Bentley hoped and wished for when he wrote the chapter 'The Future of Undercover Policing' in his memoir. Indeed, they go beyond that and demonstrate the changes in policing attitudes and a resolute commitment to engage in proactive intelligence-led policing to combat organised crime and terrorism.

We need to add that even in Seventies undercover work, the targets of investigations were aware of undercover methods. As time passes, covert operations step up, invent new tactics, use the latest technology, all to keep one step ahead of the smartest criminal enterprise. The future may involve the use of drones, negating the need for human covert policing. It is not far-fetched to suggest that criminal activities, including meetings when crimes are planned, may soon be recorded both in audio and video. It is not hard to imagine with the arrival of 'smart cities', as referenced by the head of the UK intelligence agency, GCHQ[3]. No wonder many criminals are paranoid. Even now, they will challenge innocents in a belief they may be undercover officers (UCOs). In fact, Jim Fulton did just that when telling the Operation George detectives he thought some of his neighbours in Cornwall were MI5 undercover people.

He was wrong. The "undercover people" were surrounding him, socialising with him, working with him, paying him as an employee, talking to him daily for the best part of two years. During that time, he was recorded on audio tapes, the 'product' of which eventually became the

---

[3] https://www.bbc.com/news/technology-56851558

damning evidence sending him to jail with no prospect of release for twenty-five years.

# CHAPTER 2

## Genocide

Over fifty thousand hours of conversations between William James Fulton and undercover officers engaged on Operation George were secretly recorded. In one of those recordings, Fulton said, "… They've got to shoot a Catholic once a week … about once a week and that's why they broke away. That's why the LVF broke away from the UVF was because they weren't killing enough Catholics. And the LVF wanted a Catholic per week killing."

Put yourself in the shoes of that undercover officer – how would you react to such disturbing words? These undercover officers are to be admired as the consummate professionals they truly are. They don't flinch, berate, judge or ask questions. Instead, they associate, infiltrate, befriend their target, and covertly gather the evidence for a future day of reckoning.

On the 11th of March 2021, a BBC World News article[4] reported that, "The term genocide was coined in 1943 by the Jewish-Polish lawyer Raphael Lemkin, who combined the Greek word 'genos' (race or tribe) with the Latin word 'cide' (to kill). After witnessing the horrors of the Holocaust, in which every member of his family except his brother was killed, Dr Lemkin campaigned to have genocide recognised as a crime under international law.

His efforts gave way to the adoption of the United Nations Genocide Convention in December 1948, which came into effect in

---

[4] https://www.bbc.com/news/world-11108059

January 1951. Article Two of the convention defines genocide as 'any of the following acts committed with the intent to destroy, in whole or in part, a national, ethnic, racial or *religious* [our emphasis] group …'"

This Operation George story has genocide at its centre. It's also the remarkable story of a brave, experienced, elite group of undercover officers and their forward-thinking boss, who conceptualised then executed a most brilliant plan to bring a terrorist to justice.

# CHAPTER 3

## Interview Room, Belfast

On 12 June 2001, Constable Pierce of the Devon and Cornwall Constabulary, together with a specialist armed arrest team, arrested Jim Fulton at his Plymouth home under the Prevention of Terrorism Act. To Fulton's surprise, he was flown to Belfast under armed guard in a military helicopter. His surprise turned to fear as he started to cry like a baby, dreading that he was about to be assassinated and thrown into the dark waters of the Irish Sea. By the time he had been processed at a Belfast holding centre, Fulton had reverted to type: a cocksure individual who thought he had nothing to worry about. That overconfidence was on display at the earliest stages of the disclosure interviews. Those interviews are mandatory under the umbrella of the Police and Criminal Evidence Act (PACE) and were conducted in the presence of a well-known Belfast solicitor. Fulton was settling into a chair in the stark interview room, listening closely to the introductory disclosure material articulated by an interviewing officer, undoubtedly thinking, *I'll be out of here soon.*

Then his world shattered. He rocked back on the chair, almost losing balance, whilst he took in what he had just heard: "Those people back in Plymouth. You know Neil, Robbie and the others in that firm you were working for. I must inform you they were all undercover police officers. Furthermore, they recorded your many conversations with them."

Fulton rocked forward, regaining his balance, then held his head in his hands. Once more, he started to blubber, but only for a moment. He quickly gathered himself and started to put his defence on tape – for the sake of the record.

"I mean, I thought I'd got in with a big firm in England and I just wanted to make myself more important, make myself seen that I was a big man," Jim Fulton said.

"A firm as in gangsters?" asked a detective.

"Right. So, I wanted to make myself out to be a big man."

"Right and so you decided what?"

"Just waffle."

*A firm as in gangsters?* the interviewer asked. I ask you to remember that word – 'firm' – because this is a true story about the firm that wasn't a firm at all.

Just like Jim Carrey's character in *The Truman Show,* Fulton's environment had been controlled and his life manipulated. He believed he'd been living cheek by jowl in the company of gangsters in Plymouth, England from 1999 to 2001. In fact, he'd been living in a bubble not of his own creation.

The rest of the cast in the 'firm' playing the parts of members of an organised crime group (OCG) are real enough but not genuine. They are all skilled undercover detectives and part of Operation George. This extraordinarily successful police operation was set up in the wake of the murder of the prominent human rights solicitor Rosemary Nelson in Lurgan, Northern Ireland in 1999, and therein lies the catalyst for what came later.

CHAPTER 4

## The Nelson Family Home

Monday 15 March 1999 was like any other day. The only anomaly was that Rosemary Nelson slept a little later than usual as she was feeling under the weather, partly because of how she was feeling and also because two of her children were away on a school holiday in France.

It was late morning when her friend, confidante and secretary Nuala McCann called by to find her friend still getting ready for work. They planned to have a coffee before travelling in separate cars to the law firm's office a short distance away in Lurgan town centre.

Based on the known facts, it's easy to imagine this is what happened that morning. Letting herself in with a key entrusted to her, Nuala called upstairs, "I'm here, are you ready?"

"I'll be down soon but can you do me a favour?"

"No problem. What is it?"

"Get the *Irish Times*, please. I want to read the Drumcree article and see if they published my picture."

Exchange over, Nuala went to a local newsagent to buy the paper. On her return, both women sat in the kitchen and over coffee briefly chatted about the article and their amusement at Rosemary's picture. "They never use a flattering photo, have you noticed?" Rosemary said and both women laughed.

Nuala drove to the end of a nearby road, expecting to see Rosemary driving her silver BMW past on Lake Street. Confused as to why

Rosemary hadn't passed her, Nuala drove around looking for her friend, until she came around a corner to a scene of devastation. Rosemary's BMW was a mass of twisted metal, the work of a terrorist bomb. Nuala rushed to the driver's seat. Her friend was covered in black dust and seemed gravely injured.

Nuala ran to a neighbour's house and asked her to call 999. On returning to her friend, Nuala found another neighbour, a qualified nurse, had arrived. The nurse had heard the explosion and ran to the scene. A short time later a local doctor arrived, followed by an ambulance, paramedics, the fire service, and the police. It should come as no surprise, owing to both her legs having been blown off by the blast, that medics struggled to stabilise Rosemary Nelson or relieve her pain. By the time she was cut her free from the car and taken to Craigavon

Hospital there was no more to be done to save her life. Rosemary Nelson died shortly after three o'clock that afternoon.

Later that same day, the Red Hand Defenders, a splinter Loyalist paramilitary group who some claimed was a front for the LVF, claimed responsibility for the bomb in a telephone call to the BBC Newsroom in Belfast.

This gruesome murder was a catalyst in bringing Fulton to justice for other crimes. Though there is no evidence Jim Fulton was implicated in the murder of Rosemary Nelson, he was one of many suspected who had connections to Loyalist paramilitary groups. It was her murder that acted as a mechanism for bringing him and Muriel Gibson to justice for other terrorist crimes including the murders of innocent Catholics and RUC police officers. Fulton was a Nelson murder suspect, but there is no evidence implicating him at all, even to this day.

Soon after Rosemary Nelson's death, both Fulton and Gibson fled Northern Ireland; Fulton flying to California and Gibson relocating to the West Country in England. Fulton thought he was safe. What he didn't know was that he would soon come to the notice of American law enforcement, including the FBI.

# CHAPTER 5

## California Dreaming

Murrieta is a township in Riverside County, about eighty miles south of downtown Los Angeles. Nearby Temecula is known for its wine trail and is one of the many attractions in this region of Southern California.

Muriel Gibson had connections to Murrieta. Her former husband, William Landry, and their children lived there in a battered looking yellow house. In September 1999, Jim Fulton flew to the United States then took refuge in that house together with his wife, Tanya, no doubt waiting for the hullaballoo to die down back in Belfast. But Fulton's attempts to lie low were undermined when Tanya discharged a loaded weapon in the grounds of the house. The shots rang out and were heard by some nearby brickyard workers who instinctively ducked for cover. The two workers, Johnny Buckles and Nathan Rouse, were stacking bricks with a forklift truck. Buckles later said, "Two or three shots went off. Then the fourth or fifth went zipping by us a little closer." Rouse claimed they had heard at least a dozen shots. The workers reported the shots to Murrieta police. Local law enforcement officers arrived to find the Fultons and three other adults at the home. Inside, they found two rifles, expended cartridges, ammunition, and a gun on a shelf. They also seized a .32-caliber handgun and a black T-shirt emblazoned with the slogan "Loyalist Volunteers lead the way."

A news article[5] said, "Police reported finding a number of .22 calibre rifles, an M-72 "spent" anti-tank rocket launcher, a six-inch cannon, mounted on a wooden base, two inert pipe bombs, hollowed out hand grenades with some gun powder residue, as well as 5.5 ounces of hashish and a small amount of methamphetamine."

It continued: "Police said a 33-year-old Las Vegas woman and 29-year-old Tanya Fulton admitted to having fired a handgun out a rear window of the home. Tanya Fulton's lawyer said the shooting erupted after the Las Vegas woman told his client it is legal to own firearms in the United States. The lawyer added, 'Tanya had never fired a gun, and she was told there was a big open field there and apparently a couple of shots were fired out of the window.'"

---

[5] http://www.nuzhound.com/articles/tlac1-23.htm

The Murrieta Sheriff's Department arrested the Las Vegas woman, William James (Jim) and Tanya Fulton, as well as residents Odysseus Landry, 29, and Mahatma Landry, 28, on child-endangerment, drug, and weapon charges. The child endangerment charges were levelled at Jim and Tanya Fulton owing to the presence of their two young children at the house in Murrieta. The children were taken into protective care and were returned to Northern Ireland after their parents were arrested.

The arrests took place on the 16th of December 1999, just nine months after the bomb explosion that killed Rosemary Nelson. Local law enforcement authorities in the town were notified by the FBI to put major security around Fulton almost immediately after they arrested him but were not told the reason. Many questions then started to flow about Fulton and his presence in the United States.

The US press, alerted by reports in Ireland, became aware of the implications of the case. A nationwide TV network[6] referred to Fulton and those arrested with him as a "cell of a dangerous, international Irish terrorist organization." Following that, the Californian arresting officer told the media he had not been approached by the RUC but confirmed police reports from Belfast giving details of prior convictions and other background material on the five people arrested had finally been sent to the US.

On Fulton's appearance at a court remand hearing, the District Attorney told the court the $100,000 bail being asked for each defendant was higher than the normal $5,000 per

---

[6] Ibid at 5.

defendant in such a drug case, but he declined to say why. Jail officials later said, "Regardless of whether Fulton can make bail, the immigration hold will bar his release." Fulton's California arrest caused quite a commotion at that week's official State Department briefing for journalists at the White House in Washington, with one journalist asking,[7] "What do you know about the arrest last month of a man in Southern California who is suspected of having planted a car bomb that killed Rosemary Nelson in Northern Ireland?" The terse answer from spokesman James Rubin was, "Yeah, that sounds to me like a domestic law enforcement matter, and I would refer you to the law enforcement agencies." The same article also reported that "the Assistant Chief Constable of Norfolk

---

[7] Ibid at 4 and 5.

Constabulary, Colin Port, who's heading the investigation into Nelson's murder in last year's March 15th car bombing, however, told [us] on Sunday last week that he was aware of the arrest, but had no plans to interview Fulton." Richard Harvey, a New York-based lawyer, of the Rosemary Nelson Campaign also started asking how Fulton came to be in possession of an arsenal of weapons, including explosives, and why all charges, except possession of drugs, were dramatically dropped that week. He also asked how Fulton got entry into the US and why he could remain on in contravention of immigration law. All this was going on in the background as United States Congress was holding hearings to bring pressure on the British government to hold an independent inquiry into Nelson's murder.

The explosives and weapons charges were eventually dropped, against the wishes of the local district attorney, who was controversially overruled. The district attorney and arresting officer were only informed about Fulton's loyalist connections when phoned by the *Ireland on Sunday* newspaper almost two weeks following the Murrieta arrests.

Colin Port was undoubtedly truthful but possibly disingenuous when telling the press there were no plans to interview Jim Fulton. That point was a long way off. What few people knew was that Colin Port, as head of the investigation into the Rosemary Nelson murder, had already put a covert operation in place once Muriel Gibson had been located in Plymouth, Devon, England, and after the arrest of the Fultons in California, the first phase of Operation George had commenced with the assistance of the FBI who were undoubtedly instrumental in dropping the charges against Fulton. Jim Fulton's California dreaming would soon become his nightmare.

# CHAPTER 6

## Colin Port

International pressure was building for a thorough and independent inquiry into the horrific murder of Rosemary Nelson.

As early as 17 March 1999, two days after Nelson's car was blown up, a resolution condemned the murder of Rosemary Nelson,[8] which was referred to the US House of Representatives Committee on International Relations. Amongst other things, it referred to "public knowledge that Rosemary Nelson's life was threatened on a number of occasions by the RUC Special Branch… the North's human

---

[8] https://www.govinfo.gov/content/pkg/BILLS-106hconres59ih/html/BILLS-106hconres59ih.htm

rights group, the Committee on the Administration of Justice, has called for an independent investigation into Rosemary Nelson's murder and said it would be 'untenable' for the RUC to head the inquiry… the United States should fully support the implementation of the United Nations Special Rapporteur's recommendation for an independent inquiry into the killing of Belfast lawyer Pat Finucane… calls on the United Nations to condemn these bombings and seek an independent investigation apart from the RUC; calls on the United Nations to form an independent inquiry into the harassment by the RUC of human rights lawyers and the killings of Rosemary Nelson and others."

The Good Friday Agreement (GFA), or Belfast Agreement, are two agreements, not one, but almost always referred to in the singular. They were signed on 10 April 1998, designed to end the violence of the Troubles, which had ensued since the late 1960s. It was a major development in the Northern Ireland peace process of the 1990s. Northern Ireland's present devolved system of government is based on the agreement. The agreement also created several institutions between Northern Ireland and the Republic of Ireland, and between the Republic of Ireland and the United Kingdom.

With that in mind, on the day of Rosemary Nelson's murder and recognising the need for an independent element in the murder investigation, Sir Ronnie Flanagan, then RUC Chief Constable, sought assistance from HM Inspectorate of Constabulary and the Director of the Federal Bureau of Investigation. The result was that Colin Port, the Deputy Chief Constable of Norfolk, was appointed to act as Officer in Overall Command (OIOC) of a murder investigation team (MIT) which became the most extensive murder investigation in the history of Northern Ireland.

Colin Port had spent most of his police career investigating crime, initially with the Greater Manchester Police, rising through the ranks from Detective Constable to Detective Superintendent in charge of Crime Operations and later as a Detective Chief Superintendent. He became the Head of the Criminal Investigation Department (CID) with the Warwickshire Constabulary. In 1994 he had been appointed Investigations Coordinator to the UN International Criminal Tribunal for the former Yugoslavia and in the following year Director of Investigations to the UN International Criminal Tribunal in Rwanda. In 1996 he became Head of the Southeast Regional Crime Squad. He then became Deputy Chief Constable of Norfolk. He went to Northern Ireland with a great deal of experience, particularly the targeting of serious and organised crime groups, using informants, surveillance, undercover officers and intrusive techniques.

Port was not the first to suggest that the best hope of developing a case against those suspects named in the early intelligence lay in pursuing a proactive investigation which could include both human and technical surveillance. Port had referred to it as a possibility at a meeting on 26 March 1999, when Kent police officers from England, FBI Special Agent John Guido, and senior RUC Special Branch (SB) officers, discussed 'technical issues and possible opportunities' and held a 'general discussion about intelligence versus evidence difficulties and the need to protect intelligence gathering tactics whilst exploring every opportunity to secure evidence in this very important case'. Owing to internal RUC politics, it was clear the SB had some reservations about such a course.

However, in the latter half of 1999, significant opportunities arose which enabled the MIT to initiate surveillance without the assistance of SB, using techniques that were less familiar to those targeted and at times and in places when they were almost certainly less watchful. These opportunities arose when two of the murder suspects left Northern Ireland. In September 1999 one of them, William James ('Jim') Fulton, travelled to the USA; another, Muriel Gibson, moved from Portadown, initially to Plymouth and later Cornwall in England. When Jim Fulton returned from the USA to Northern Ireland, he was warned that a threat had been made against his life and so he also moved to Cornwall, where he resided temporarily with Muriel Gibson before finding accommodation of his own. From time to time during the following months both Jim Fulton and Muriel Gibson were visited by others whom the Port MIT regarded as suspects involved in Rosemary Nelson's murder.

Port was also familiar with the CHIS – covert human intelligence source – database back in England. It was originally planned to establish a single database containing details of undercover police officers and confidential informants ('snouts', as they were informally known). That idea was scrapped, resulting in a separate database of nationally accredited undercover officers (UCOs). With Gibson's new location in Plymouth and Fulton's return in mind, Port and others started collating a list of experienced Level 1 undercover officers, those with deep infiltration experience. This list contained the details of the undercover officers who would soon form two teams on the covert intelligence operation, code named George.

CHAPTER 7

## Down the Rabbit Hole

Unlike in the pioneering undercover cop days of Operation Julie, covert policing is now highly regulated, whether using human or technical resources. If the rules and regulations are broken, even bent or twisted a little, any evidence gleaned is certain to be ruled inadmissible in court hearings. The modern undercover officer is trained to 'open doors', in that a target or suspect is unwittingly put in a situation where they have a genuine choice to talk about past or future crimes or voluntarily offer up vital intelligence which may or may not be potential evidence.

The target cannot be subjected to questioning, otherwise the provisions of Code C of the Police and Criminal Evidence Act 1984 (PACE) come into play. The real issue is whether the undercover officers conducted an interview; in English law that means a conversation including questioning regarding an offence. Answers received by UCs not having cautioned a target who is now a suspect may, depending on the judge, not be used in court as evidence.

The preparation for any operation involves the UCO meeting with his boss to work out the parameters. All sanctioned actions on the part of any UCO are signed off in advance. In that way, the UCOs know exactly how far they are lawfully allowed to go within each step of the operation.

Elite Level 1 officers know and live by a rule of not disturbing a pre-existing environment. They do not act like a bull in a china shop because if they do targets are more likely to suspect them and no one will trust them. It becomes a long-term process when infiltrating an organised crime group (OCG). In that way, it increases the chances of obtaining the information necessary to prosecute the gang members.

Now that Colin Port had a list of elite UCOs, how best to deploy them against the targets of Jim Fulton and Muriel Gibson?

Through close liaison with the FBI, Port and the embryo Operation George team (which by now was a spin-off from the Rosemary Nelson murder investigation) learnt Fulton was to be deported from the United States back to the United Kingdom. The team realised its best chances of infiltrating the Fulton/Gibson axis – a cabal of two – was to ensure Fulton did not reside in Northern Ireland where the recognised surveillance problems could prevent the effectiveness of any attempted infiltration. Besides, Port's list of UCOs was full of cops from England, though not necessarily English. Embedding them in Ulster would have been both futile and presented a grave risk to their personal security.

What happened next was a master stroke by any standards. One undercover team consisting of a man and a woman was deployed in Cornwall with the brief to establish themselves in the local community. They were known as Dave S and Sam, and they set about starting up a small business as market traders in Camborne.

Liz, another UCO, was deployed to Plymouth where Gibson had been located. Liz was tasked with making the first approach to Gibson in a natural way. As you will see, she succeeded. Eventually, Liz paved the way for Muriel Gibson to tell Jim Fulton that Liz's fella, who was another UCO called Neil, was looking for a driver.

Simultaneously, someone or possibly more than one person whispered into Jim Fulton's ear whilst he was still in California, "You want to think twice about where to go when you get back to the UK."

"Why?" Fulton asked.

"There's a story doing the rounds, you're on a hit list back in Belfast."

Was one of the whisperers someone from the FBI? Your guess is as good as ours, but we know they were actors on the stage at this time and close to Port's MIT. It's also known that Fulton was covertly recorded whilst in custody in the United States when he denied killing Rosemary Nelson to a fellow prisoner. That sounds like the FBI.

That same 'story' may have also been fed to Muriel Gibson, who would undoubtedly pass it on to Fulton, probably through his lawyer in the States or her kids in Murrieta. It's an educated guess the 'rumour' was deliberately started at the instigation of Port, who utilised the array of law enforcement and security services in Belfast and elsewhere to propagate the rumour throughout all the loyalist haunts. The Metropolitan Police Service (MPS or Met) Special Branch also played its part. Dame Stella Rimington, former Director General of the Security Service, explained in a lecture[9] how "Special Branches [act] as the main interface between the Security Service and the Police

---

[9] https://www.mi5.gov.uk/cy/node/412

Service as a whole." The Met's SB has responsibility for policing Heathrow and other major ports. Have you ever noticed the man in plain clothes standing close to the passport control booths at the airport? You know, the guy with the frown. The chances are he's Special Branch and keeping a close eye on arrivals. One did when Fulton arrived at Heathrow and took him to a nearby interview room where Fulton once more was told about a death threat. Despite the reinforcement of the message, Fulton carried on and returned to Belfast, undoubtedly because he wished to be reunited with his wife and children who had all returned from California at an earlier time.

Nonetheless, Fulton and his family did return to England after he had spent one month in his County Armagh hangouts, owing to a combination of unease on his part and Gibson telling him about a golden opportunity. All these initial steps were part of creating an 'open door', inviting Fulton to walk in and join his friend Muriel Gibson to 'disappear down the rabbit hole'. In the controlled vacuum created by Operation George, the task would be to create an environment in which Fulton and Gibson would talk freely about events in Northern Ireland.

Some of the players in the Operation George sting would soon be in place, but it would be a long way from the denouement, one which draws comparisons with the movie *The Sting*. The title refers to the moment when a con artist finishes the "play" and takes the mark's money. If a con is successful, the mark does not realize he has been cheated until the con men are long gone, if at all.

*The Sting*? The *Truman Show*? *Alice in Wonderland*? Get the picture? Pun intended.

# CHAPTER 8

## Liz

The first thing Liz knew about Operation George was late September 1999, when Trevor in the Undercover Office called her asking if she, "Fancied a bit of work?" That was a question she had been asked many times before, owing to her lengthy experiences of undercover roles infiltrating criminal gangs.

"Oh yeah, what is it this time, a handbag on the arm of … let me guess…"

Trev cut across her. "No Liz, this is a proper bit of work. It does not come without a slice of risk, and you'll be working alone initially. I can't say anything more now over the phone – the boss wants you to come into the office for a sit-down chat tomorrow at two. Can you make it?"

"Bloody hell, Trev, you know how to get a girl excited. Two it is!" Liz killed the call and carried on completing the report she was crafting about her latest deployment. Liz was a seasoned UCO who had worked on infiltrations for many years across the UK. This next role was different: rather than a gang, there was just one person's world she was to infiltrate.

At five to two the next day she walked into the Cover Office and acknowledged Trev with a nod and a swift hello. Trev, just finishing off the final touches to three coffees, asked, "No sugar, right?"

"Right, no sugar, what's the job about, mate?"

"I honestly can't say a word. I've been sworn to secrecy, as will you in a minute. The boss is on the phone as we speak. When he's finished, we're in and everything will be made clear. But I can tell you this: it's fucking big and you have been handpicked."

Liz grabbed her brew and sat at the nearest empty desk. She knew she wouldn't be disturbed by its regular occupant, Sam, as she was out on the plot in another part of the UK working a market stall with Dave, usually known as Dave S, owing to Dave being a common name for UCOs.

After a few minutes, the boss's door opened and Len, the gaffer, crossed the office to Liz and greeted her with a handshake and invited her and Trev into his office. Making his way to his desk, he said, "Right, Liz, what's Trev told you about this bit of work?"

Settling into a chair, Liz avoided eye contact with the boss until the last few syllables of his question. "Zero, nothing, nada, jack shit, boss,

OPERATION GEORGE · 53

other than there is a bit of risk wrapped round it and I'm on my own. So apart from that, nothing, boss."

Satisfied, the boss took his seat behind his sparsely furnished desktop decorated with only a landline telephone, a mobile phone, and a twenty-pack of Silk Cut cigarettes besides a lighter inscribed: 'To Len, best of luck on your promotion.' From a drawer, he pulled out a chunky blue folder marked 'Operation George.' On setting down the folder, his piercing eyes locked on to Liz's. "Good, and that's how we're going to play this one, Liz. Before I go any further, what have you got in your diary for the next three to six months?"

Liz knew this wasn't an unusual question for a UCO to be asked when there is the possibility of a bit of work on the table. Undercover officers are like every other grown-up on the planet;

they have stuff they have to deal with in their private, home and working life. Liz was no exception to this rule. She had a fella, Tommy, who wasn't a cop but was supportive in her chosen role. He knew there were times that she would be away on a job for prolonged periods of time. Contact wasn't easy. He couldn't just pick up his phone and call her throw-away phone from his mobile or house phone. That would leave a footprint on Liz's phone record which in time could be pored over by a defence team of barristers. Her job phone or personal mobile would be switched off and held by her Cover Officer when she was on the plot. To keep a line of communication open for emergency, Liz always ensured that Tommy had a list of the first names of the Cover Officers and their job mobile numbers, just in case. Tommy knew the Cover team from downtown piss-ups and barbeques in the back gardens of their homes. He was trusted and part of the undercover family and therefore looked after by all the team members.

So, family life and potential issues. No issues. Tick that box.

The job Liz had just finished would take more than six months to get anywhere near the Crown Court and if she, the Operational Team and the Crown Prosecution Services (CPS) had done their jobs correctly, her role should have been protected under Public Interest Immunity (PII[10]). However, there was always the chance that she could be called for a closed-door hearing with the trial judge over a part of her submitted evidence and or role. You can't call

---

[10] Public Interest Immunity or PII as it is often called; previously known as Crown privilege, is a principle of English common law under which the English courts can grant a court order allowing one litigant to refrain from disclosing evidence to the other litigants where disclosure would be damaging to the public interest.

the odds on that, and you just have to roll with it.

So, work issues. None. Tick.

Privately, Liz was thinking of settling down to a more stable lifestyle and maybe sitting the promotion exam to boost her pension and to share her knowledge and experience with the new breed of police officers who were prepared to enter this challenging and exciting world of undercover policing. *Well*, Liz thought, *another six months isn't going to make that much of a difference.*

So, private issues. None. Tick.

Breaking free from her thoughts, Liz said, "Just finishing off my report and exxies [expense claims] from the last op, boss. A week away with Tommy, it was going to be two weeks, but he's arranged and paid for a trip to Spain golfing with his mates because he didn't expect me home for another couple of weeks. Typical. So, I'm all yours. What you got, boss?"

"What I've got in this folder is 'Operation George'. This is going to be a trail blazer. Never have UK Police Plc done anything like this, it's unique. What you are about to hear doesn't leave this office. I'll give you an outline without going into detail because if you don't fancy it, no worries, walk away and no one will think less of you. But before going into the finer detail, I have to know that you want this job."

Liz looked at Trev and then at Len with a frown. "Bloody hell, you're asking me to sign up for a job you've told me nothing about. I can walk away, no bother. I'll be working alone and there is, in your words, a slice of risk. Where is it and what is it, can you tell me that?"

"Okay," said Len and then, after a slight pause, "there is a female in the West Country that we want you to befriend. She is of great interest to several UK law enforcement agencies. She is the key to an international operation, and we need someone to turn that key. That someone could just be you, Liz. In or out?"

Not one for using bad language in front of the boss but having a full vocabulary when needed and appropriate, Liz responded, "For fuck's sake, I'm none the wiser but you have got my complete and undivided attention. Count me in on this once in a lifetime opportunity. I'm intrigued and a hundred percent in. Now for god's sake, tell me what the fuck it's all about."

The atmosphere in the boss's office lightened and Len opened the file. He began, "Operation George is a deep undercover operation. It is a post-murder enquiry into the killing of a prominent Catholic solicitor, Ms Rosemary Nelson. The murder took place in Northern

Ireland on 15 March 1999. We suspect the LVF. One of their members, Muriel Gibson, has left Northern Ireland and taken up residence in a bed and breakfast in Plymouth."

There was enough in this short summary to get Liz's mind working. She snapped off three questions: "Do we have a plan? Who am I working for? Who's my cover?"

Trev replied without hesitation, "I'm going to cover, and I've got an idea of a plan about why you have just suddenly dropped out of the sky. I have read the file inside out, backwards forwards and upside down and there is stuff in there that you don't need to know. Trust me."

"Always," Liz replied.

Trev continued, "You know your safety is paramount at all times and I won't hold back on any info that compromises that. But there is stuff we'd rather you found out for yourself by getting close to Gibson and winning over her confidence."

"Yeah, I get that, and I much prefer it coming from the target, then my reaction to it is very natural. Who am I working for?"

Len took over. "This is a Royal Ulster Constabulary job being run out of Northern Ireland. the OIOC [Officer in Overall Command] is Deputy Chief Constable Colin Port from Norfolk Old Bill. Port is a top, top, cop, career detective with some big jobs under his belt; he's been appointed head of the investigation."

Liz looked somewhat puzzled. "Excuse me for asking, but why is the DCC of Norfolk heading up a job for the RUC?"

Len looked across at Liz with an eyebrow raised. "That's a good question, Liz. Let's just put that down to politics and park that there for the mo, mate."

"Okay. What's my way into this Muriel Gibson of Plymouth, pray tell?" asked Liz.

"How do you feel about escaping a domestic situation, Liz, as a cover story? That could explain why you have moved into B&B accommodation," Trev said.

"Yeah, I can work something around that, let's build on it a bit more. I don't want to appear vulnerable or a pushover to this target. Been there, done that, too many pitfalls. We need to be thinking two steps ahead so let's not open doors for her. I'll take the domestic angle but not violence; I don't really want to appear a victim. How about the domestic thing is I'm married and having a relationship with a guy, long term relationship, and we're looking at taking it to the next level and leaving my other half is the next step. That's why I'm in Plymouth, and it will give me an excuse for going on the missing list now and then. Dirty weekend away with my fella! I'm liking the sound of this bit of work now."

Trev chipped in with a touch of caution in his voice. "Easy, Liz, it's only make believe and Tommy's a mate. I get your point about appearing vulnerable and a victim. So shagging, notionally of course, mate, some fella from Plymouth might be a good line to run out. Yeah, I like that, and it gives us some flexibility on the plot."

"Listen, Liz,' Len said, 'this job, this bit of work, *it will be,* and *you will be* tightly controlled and directed. Every idea you come up with or we come up with, every next move you want to make, has got to be given the green light by the Op Team. There is no fucking about with that. You are going to be a cog in a machine. There is stuff going on here, over in Ireland and in other places, a lot of moving parts. It's a bit like three-dimensional chess, and Colin Port and his team can see the whole of the board and they decide what piece moves next and where it moves to. I can't stress that enough, Liz."

Liz sucked up a lung full of air then exhaled. "Wow! What about going to the loo? Do I need permission, or can we assume that's a given?" Both men smiled as she continued, "No, seriously boss if you say jump, I'll ask how high before I take off. I trust you guys to look after me and to watch my back, if you're happy with what's going on I'm totally relaxed about it."

The next steps were put in motion over the next few days, the three of them having further meetings to plan it all.

Liz was going to use one of her covert identities that was locked away in a secure steel cabinet bolted to the floor and wall inside the office. She picked out a sealed brown envelope with the name Liz Taylor written across the front. Tipping the contents out, she checked the driving licence and refreshed her memory with the address and postcode. There were also a Lloyds Bank debit and credit card in the same name registered to the same address as the driving licence. A Tesco club card, B&Q loyalty card in the name of Taylor, half a book of postage stamps and a Costa Coffee loyalty card made up the remainder of the contents of the Liz Taylor alias. She gathered them up and placed them into the various pockets and compartments of an empty designer purse she had picked up at a car boot sale a few weeks earlier for a couple of quid. *I knew this was a good buy*, she thought. Trev gave her £180 in various notes from the cash box which Liz stuffed into the YSL purse together with some coins from her own purse. Trevor then picked up a couple of Undercover Officers' Notebooks and secured them in his own rucksack.

"We haven't mentioned a car. What am I going to use as transport, Trev?" Liz enquired of her Cover Officer.

"Your car is being fitted out as we speak. They had a bit of a technical issue with a piece of kit and the hard wiring or something. The guy did explain it to me, but it was all rocket science to me and went straight over my nut. It's coming, don't worry, might not be here till next week. I'll drop you by the train station and you can get a cab from there."

"Why can't we just wait a week, Trev?"

"They want you on the ground this week, Liz. Remember what the boss said: three-dimensional chess. On another point, this fella you've left home for, has he got a name?"

"A name? 'Course he's got a name!"

"What is it?" Trev said.

Liz thought, Keep the lie as close to the truth as possible, easy to remember that way.

"Before me and Tommy got together, I had a fling with a guy who would have given his world for me, but the timing wasn't right. He was called Neil. So, let's call my fella Neil," she said.

"Okay. They want you to give Neil the profile of a wealthy businessman who has his fingers into several pies. The sort of guy that on the face of it looks hundred percent legit. Neil plays his cards close to his chest, but he's got properties and business interests in the UK and Europe. Don't go into detail about Neil's business, but make sure you let Muriel think he's not a straight runner, that he has an edge to him."

"Is this the new man in my life then? He'd better not be a minger or a fat bastard. I've got standards, Trev, and I'm not dropping them for Colin Port," Liz said.

Both officers laughed and finished off their preparations. Trev tossed a box towards Liz that contained her new throw-away phone. Trev had paid cash for the phone from a phone shop out of the area and paid for the call credit in the same way. It wasn't traceable to any individual.

"Here you are, Liz. I've plumped my new number in under Trev, the rest is up to you to download apps and numbers. You don't want to look like billy-no-mates on the plot, do you?"

Liz took the phone out of the box and discarded everything other than the charger and the USB connector. "Where did you get this, Trev? Toys 'R' Us? It's a piece of crap, mate, and the colour is awful. Why couldn't you let me get my own phone?"

"The op team needed your number on the hurry up. Sorry about the colour, Liz, but it suits your eyes," Trev said.

"It's bright red, Trev."

"As I said, it suits your eyes."

Liz shook her head and said in her best West Country accent, "Wanker!"

Trev, laughing, said, "It's the West Country you're heading for. So why the fuck are you speaking Welsh?"

"Wanker!" Liz repeated in what she believed was a West Country accent, but there was no discernible difference between both attempts.

# CHAPTER 9

## Exeter

The next morning Trev and Liz travelled to a hotel just outside of Exeter and went straight to room 26. On arrival at the room, Trev gave a soft tap. The door opened for Liz to see a man who was a stranger to her. She later found out his name was Barry. It was clear from the greeting that Trev and Barry had met before, and Liz speculated they had met and had numerous phone calls leading up to this meeting. On entering the room, Liz saw another woman who stood to approach Liz and introduced herself as Kate, and then busied herself with arranging hot drinks. Liz was under the impression that Barry outranked Kate and herself. Not that it was any big deal, for Liz knew, as did all experienced UCOs, it's your role not your rank that dictates your status in the group. Barry informed the small group they were just waiting for the Detective Inspector (DI) to arrive.

It was the DI's job to brief Liz and issue her with a Pocket Notebook (PNB): a process that all in the room had taken part in before. There was a lot of small talk going on about this and that but nothing about Liz's deployment. This weighed on Liz's mind a bit, but not to the point of 'what the fuck, can we talk about the elephant in the room'. She knew this was different to anything else she had been involved with before and started to realise that she was the key, the starter cog of what was clearly going to be a long job. Liz had been deployed on infiltrations before, but always with a partner. This was different. She was going to be gathering evidence and not intelligence. That evidence would have to be eventually transformed into reams of typed transcripts of covert recordings suitable to put in front of a judge. She was to work alone and knew that first in was the most difficult part of any undercover operation. You fail then the job fails.

After another soft tap at the door a young guy who introduced himself as Andy Stevens entered. Liz correctly guessed that he was the DI. A mug of coffee was pushed his way and there were smiles all round. Liz was expecting an Irish accent, but this guy was a cockney. He gave the room an up-to-date briefing on the operation so far. Muriel Gibson was living in the B&B; she used the phone box at the end of the street once a week on a Wednesday at around six pm. She enjoyed a game of bingo on a Thursday night. Her favoured café was 'Beach Cafe' where she would go to for a sandwich with coffee during the day and read trash mags. Muriel had found herself a local drug dealer who was known to police for supplying class 'B' Cannabis and Class 'A' Cocaine and Ecstasy. She was also obtaining drugs on prescription from her doctor.

Liz thought, This is going to be challenging – a pot smoking, pill popping, bingo nut who reads fucking trash mags.

Many outside of the police force, and even some inside it, think that undercover work is sexy and high adrenaline stuff. Liz, on hearing about her target, would have begged to differ. Andy continued his briefing, treading carefully so as not to give Liz information that she would not need. "Your job is to befriend Gibson and let her talk. See what she says. Record it and bring it back to me. Remember, this is a post murder inquiry. Be careful when you engage her in conversation that you don't interview her. Let her talk. It's not your job to question her about any criminal offences. Code C and PACE always apply. I repeat, always. Clear, Liz?"

"Clear, boss," Liz said.

Andy continued, "The guy Neil, your fella. Just gently introduce him by name and that you and he are close. Leave Gibson with the impression he's a bit of a gangster type of guy. Don't go too deep into it. We just want him painted into the background at this time in case we can work something in later. Okay?"

"Got it boss, no problem," Liz said.

Trev crossed the room and handed Liz her recording device and a supply of tapes. "That will keep you going for a while, Liz," he said as she took the equipment from him.

The boss produced photographs of Gibson. They were a mixture of surveillance and mug shots. Liz made a mental image in her head of Gibson's face. *Never to be forgotten*. The DI concluded by informing Liz that there was a 'Vacancy' sign in the window of the B & B right now. Liz thought, *Bite the bullet, girl, and go get yourself a bed for the night.* Then she said, "Right then, let's get this show on the road." Liz looked towards Andy and asked if he had a phone number of the B&B. "I'll try booking a room over the phone," she said to no one in particular.

Liz took herself off and, sitting in Trevor's car on the car park outside, she made the call. The phone in the B&B was answered by a female who introduced herself as Marie. Liz enquired about any vacancies and the cost and was booked into room 3 within minutes. "Yeah, Liz Taylor, thanks. I'll see you soon, thank you so much, you're a godsend, Marie." Liz finished her call and returned to the hotel room. She updated the group and started to write her notes in a PNB given to her by Trev. She recorded that she had been briefed by DI Stevens; she had seen photographs identified by their exhibit marks and made a phone call to the B&B; she had then spoken with Marie and booked into room 3. The boss signed off the notes, as did Liz, and handed the book back to Trev for safe keeping.

When the meeting broke up, Liz and Trev got into Trev's car. Liz handed over her job and personal mobile phones, and handbag containing her real life. Trevor placed the items into his rucksack and checked that Tommy had his number if needed. "Yeah, he's got it, do me a favour will you? Just drop him a text every day or so and let him know I'm alive and kicking mate, ta," Liz said.

"As always, mate," he replied. Trev dropped Liz off outside the train station. Just before she got out of the car they agreed on a safe word or phrase: something the UCO could use in a telephone conversation without attracting attention from others. It would alert the Cover Officer that the UCO was in danger of some kind and needed extracting immediately. It was essential the word or phrase had to fit into a normal conversation. They decided on, 'What fucking sunshine?'

Liz stood outside the train station with her suitcase. Just in case someone had noticed her getting out of the car, she made her way into the ticket hall and bought a newspaper, then made her way into the buffet bar for a coffee. She was now alone and about to enter the world of a terrorist, Muriel Gibson. She thought for a moment about the people sat around her. What would they think if they knew she was an undercover police officer, deployed against a Northern Irish Terrorist? These people were just going about their daily routine, but there she was amongst them, a lone female on a dangerous deployment. None of them knew the real Liz, who had a four-bedroom detached house in Middle England, took expensive holidays with the love of her life, organised barbeques in her back garden and got pissed with girlfriends on a Saturday night. Like all experienced UCOs, Liz was now in role, dismissing all thoughts of her personal life, and started to look forward to a cheap B&B in Plymouth.

It was a short journey on the train from Exeter to Plymouth. On arriving at Plymouth, she walked out of the station towards the taxi rank. From there, she took a cab to her new home. She paid the driver while still seated in the back seat. Once out of the cab, she put her throw-away burner phone to her ear with one hand and activated her recording device with the other. Liz didn't know who she would run into when she entered the B&B. It could possibly be Muriel Gibson. So, on went the device. The first of many recordings that Operation George would generate.

Tape one. Day one.

Liz was greeted by the lady she had spoken to on the phone. "Is it Liz?" she asked.

"Yeah, that's me, and you must be Marie, pleased to meet you and thanks for doing this at short notice."

Marie gave Liz the keys to room 3 and directed her towards the first floor. Once in the room Liz gave it the quick once over. It was clean, spacious and had a window that looked out over the street. *First things first, let's find a hide for the tricky stuff,* she thought. The room had an ensuite. Liz managed to pull the plastic trim away from under the shower tray which provided an ideal place to stash her recorder and tapes.

The first week Liz made sure she visited the 'Beach Café' every day to build up a relationship and legend with the café staff. She addressed Pauline behind the counter as if she had gone to school with her. "Morning Liz, coffee no sugar?" Pauline would call out as Liz walked in.

*Job done, I'm a local, well as far as Pauline is concerned.* Liz hinted about her complicated love life when chatting with Pauline, knowing that the gossip would spread Liz's story around the café and local community. Liz knew that was good trade craft. She also fostered the habit of taking a jog along the sea front at around six most evenings. Her route took her along the coastline, passing a public phone box at the end of the street near to the B&B.

In a constant state of readiness, Liz always carried her recording device ready to activate if she saw Gibson, just in case there was a chance of a verbal exchange. On two occasions in the first week she acknowledged a female who was waiting outside the phone box, who had commented on her running. The woman spoke with an Irish accent. As Liz got closer and recognised Gibson, she switched on the device, believing a wasted tape is better than a missed opportunity, but that opportunity had not

yet presented itself. One week went by and Liz and Gibson never crossed paths in the B&B. Liz was taking the opportunity to download her daily events to Trev via the burner phone on her early evening runs. She thought, *A slow start, but that's the best way. Only fools rush in.*
But then on a Thursday morning Liz popped down for a light breakfast of tea and toast in the breakfast room of the B&B. She was a little later than usual and found the room busy. Gibson was sitting at a table in the bay window with a free seat to her left. *Device on and into the room.* "Hi, do you mind if I join you?" Liz said.

"No, for sure I'd enjoy the company, come on sit yourself down," Gibson replied. *First contact.*
"I'm Liz, how are you doing?"
"Oh, you know, good days and bad days. Today looks like it might be a good day," Muriel said in

that strong, unmistakeable Northern Irish accent.

Liz thought, Yeah, good day for me, but a shit day for you, love.

Muriel mentioned that she had seen Liz around the place and didn't want to intrude because she seemed preoccupied. Liz didn't push the relationship and reacted to Gibson's comments with, "Well, you know what they say, men…you can't live with them, and you can't live without them."

Muriel laughed. "I could give you lessons in men, love."

The new friends continued with social chit chat. After breakfast, the two women went their own way. Liz had signed up at the local leisure centre that was equipped with a pool and gym. *The job was paying so let's enjoy it* was her motto. The rest of her days were filled by walking around the city centre, window shopping, or reading a good book on Plymouth Hoe, the large south-facing open public space. It was impossible not to think of her real life during the 'idle hours.'

The arrangements around this deployment effectively meant Liz had no real life for the first two weeks. But Tommy would be home soon from his trip abroad. She contacted Trev and asked if she could clear the plot early on Thursday. Trevor suggested he pick her up at the drop off point on Wednesday after breakfast, and they could make their way to the hotel in Exeter for a bottle of vino and a meal, followed by a debrief on Thursday, and then Liz was free for a long weekend.

When an undercover officer says he or she worked undercover for five or ten years or more, it does not mean they worked undercover for three hundred and sixty-five days every year of their undercover career. All UCOs all have a life outside the job. Liz was no different. So, with the offer of a long weekend on the table there was no contest. "Yeah, that sounds like a plan, Trev, let's do it. Dinner's on you. Cheers, mate."

# CHAPTER 10

## Cornwall

The following day, Liz was sitting on Plymouth Hoe reading a romantic paperback she had picked up in one of the charity shops. Always aware of her surroundings, she noticed Gibson heading her way. *Bang. On went the recorder.* Liz knew that Gibson would stop and chat.

"How's it going, Liz?"

"Oh, hi, Muriel," Liz said with nonchalance before adding, "Yeah, it's going as good as it can be. What about you?"

Muriel sat down on the bench next to Liz, looking out to sea. "I've been down the council banging the desk about getting a house. That

B&B is driving me fucking nuts. Apparently, the council here have an agreement with other councils, and I could end up in a place in Devon, Dorset, Somerset or Cornwall, which ever one comes up first. What about yourself, love?"

"I'm in a different situation to you, Muriel. I've got a house, but I can't live in it any more with him. It's a long story for another time maybe."

"Don't worry love, Pauline in the café mentioned you had men problems. We've all been there. If you ever need a friend to just talk to, I'm here for you, love."

"That's kind of you, Muriel, thanks. My sister has invited me down for a few days. I might take her up on it. Her husband is away working, and we can have some girlie time."

"That's the spirit, love, get yourself off and have a change of scenery for a few days, it will do you the world of good. I'm off to the Beach Café for a late dinner or an early tea. I'll see you later, love." With that, Muriel stood up and walked off in the direction of the café.

That is one of the fundamental bits of trade craft a UCO must develop. It's okay having a story about what you're doing in a place and where you came from. What you must have, is a believable and sustainable reason on why you disappear every now and then. "Where do you go to?" is a common question. So, you've got to have a reason why you disappear. UCOs all have a normal life with the same demands as everyone else. So, Liz dropped her sister into the mix.

Liz switched off the device, smiling inwardly, and continued reading her book. She thought, *I've got something for the op team. Contact made, looking at moving, could be Devon,*

*Cornwall Somerset or even Dorset.* Liz picked a bottle of half decent red and dinner from the Co-op on the way back to her room. She planned an early night curled up watching TV in her room and finishing her book. What Liz was not aware of, owing to the sterile corridors[11] of undercover work, was that the operational team was already lining up accommodation for Gibson in Cornwall where she would become a neighbour to Dave S and Sam.

The following morning, Liz missed her tea and toast and waited to see Muriel leave the B&B, heading off in the direction of town. Liz had her bag ready to go and called a cab. She had some time to kill so grabbed a coffee and a *Sun* newspaper – not her preference but she was in character and the *Sun* seemed like the right

---

[11] Sterile corridors in covert policing means forms of cut-offs based on a 'need to know' policy.

paper. Within half an hour she would be back in her normal world with normal people enjoying normal things. She stepped out of the cab and walked into the station. Arriving in Exeter, she knew Trev would call so she could sit and relax. Five minutes later her phone rang. "I'm outside, Liz," the familiar voice said.

"On my way," Liz said.

Trev's BMW was waiting in the pick-up bay. She threw her bag on the back seat and jumped into the front passenger seat and greeted Trev with, "All right mate, get me the fuck out of here."

Trev had booked two double rooms across the corridor from each other. He'd use his room for the debrief the following day. He handed Liz her PNB so she could record her activities over the week without going into too much detail. The tape was the contemporaneous record of all meetings with Gibson. All Liz had to do was record each of the tapes as exhibits and the onward continuity to preserve the integrity of the exhibits. The last thing to do was her exxies. Once completed, a shower, change of gear, and an early bottle of vino in some wine bar rubbing shoulders with city slickers. The type who told everyone that they had the best job in the world. Little did they know that the unassuming couple stood next to them, Liz and Trev, led a far more exciting life than they could even dream of.

Both officers retired for the night at around ten o'clock and were dressed, fed and watered for the eleven o'clock debriefing the following morning. Liz and Trev were waiting in the hotel room for the Op team and DI to arrive. Bang on time there was a gentle tapping on the door. The team of three walked in, headed by Andy

Stevens with Barry taking up the rear. Liz verbally debriefed the team on the events of the week. She handed the recordings (Product) to Kate and recorded the fact in her PNB and then handed the book to Andy to sign off.

"Any mention of Neil yet?" Andy asked.

"No not yet, boss, but I've dropped the hint my reason for being here is man trouble. She has offered to lend a sympathetic ear if I need one. I didn't want to push it too hard in the first week or so."

"No complaint here Liz," said Andy, "you've done great. The relationship between you and Gibson will grow. I'm sure of that.'

# CHAPTER 11

## Lizzie

The next few weeks saw Liz spending more and more time with Muriel, who began to talk about her life in Northern Ireland and the USA. Muriel would often smoke cannabis in Liz's company. On one of the first occasions Muriel offered Liz a draw. Knowing it was bound to happen, Liz was geared up with her excuse.

"Fancy a wee bit yourself, Lizzie?" asked Muriel.

"Not for me darling. I had a bad turn with it once. When I was young, I suffered from asthma. I had all kinds of medications, hormone treatments and inhalers, you name it. It was really bad. And you know how it goes when you try things when you're young. Well, I nearly died. Honest, I had to go to hospital and get put on a breathing machine. I nearly bloody died. So that was it for me, never again. So, thanks but no thanks, you crack on, love."

That was it. Muriel never offered Lizzie, as Muriel now called her, a draw again.

As the relationship developed, Liz spoke more and more about her fella, Neil. She told Muriel how she would go off for weekends or a few days in the week with him, telling her tales of trips up to London enjoying the shops and the night life, and how Neil was very good to her, spending a lot of money on her. These notional trips with Neil gave Liz a believable and sustainable reason for her not being on the plot. In truth, they gave Liz down time to be with Tommy. Over the Christmas and New Year period the story went that Neil took Liz off to a castle in Scotland. To bolster this story, Liz purportedly sent Muriel a postcard of Loch Ness wishing her a Merry Christmas and Happy New Year. A Scottish UCO, belonging to the now defunct Scottish Crime and Drug Enforcement Agency, and Trev's friend, had bought the card and posted it from Scotland at Trev's request, but not before Liz had written the message and signed it. It was then handed over to Trev who posted it to his Scottish UCO friend who then did his bit in the subterfuge.

When in Liz's company, Muriel began to open up about her involvement with a paramilitary organisation. She spoke about her many associates within this group, one of whom was a guy called Jimmy. Owing to a 'need to know' protocol, only the most senior officers would realise the significance of Gibson's revelations.

At that time, Liz was unaware Jimmy was William James Fulton, leader of the LVF in Portadown. On the first debrief when Liz attended and mentioned the guy 'Jimmy' there was no reaction from the Op Team or Cover Officer. It was recorded in the debrief note in the usual manner and even regarded by Kate as an insignificant bit of info. At the end of the debriefing, Andy again thanked Liz for her work and instructed her to continue in the same vein using the same tactics. However, Liz couldn't continue to live in the B&B forever. It didn't look right, plus Gibson was about all day and every day. It didn't fit the picture Liz painted of her boyfriend, Neil. So, after about six weeks Liz moved out of the B&B and into one of Neil's flats that had supposedly recently become available and freshly decorated.

Of course, Liz told Muriel she was free to call in for a catch up and a coffee anytime. After all, Liz and Muriel were now good friends. Their relationship was on solid ground and Muriel trusted Liz with some stories about her activities across the water and her friend, Jimmy. Liz continued to debrief on Jimmy's involvement in terrorism in Northern Ireland and the team continued to record her information without a flicker of interest. Later, after learning the truth, Liz told Kate that she would never play poker with her.

## Dave S and Sam

About this time, Muriel had been offered a house in Camborne, Cornwall. The local authority told her that if she refused the move, she would be placed at the bottom of the list and it might be a further six months before she received another offer. Muriel agreed to view the property and was driven down to Camborne by a member of the relevant department. The house was in a nice location and freshly decorated. The couple living next door were out doing some gardening when Muriel turned up. Not shy at coming forward, Muriel called out towards the couple in her Northern Irish brogue.

"How you doing? Looks like we might be neighbours."

Both stopped what they were doing and walked towards the fence between the two houses.

"Pleased to meet you, I'm Dave and this is Sam."

"Good to meet you," Sam said shaking Muriel's hand.

"I'm Muriel, it seems nice and quiet around here, no noisy kids and barking dogs."

Dave went on to say there were some young kids, but they were well behaved and the guy across the way had a Lab that was as soft as shit. Muriel was satisfied and agreed to take the place, then made the arrangements to move from Plymouth to Camborne in Cornwall, which are about sixty miles apart. Whilst she was making those arrangements pending her relocation, the Op Team got busy, applying for authorities to deploy probes, and then fitting without attracting the attention of the neighbours. Well, not all the neighbours. Dave and Sam knew what was going on. They had been patiently waiting for this day since they were first deployed to Camborne.

At a briefing soon after Muriel's trip to Camborne, Liz was instructed to mention to Muriel that Neil had recently lost one of his trusted drivers. The driver had suffered a heart attack and wouldn't be fit for work for some time or maybe never again. The story, according to Liz, was this situation was giving Neil some stress because this guy was trusted and a loyal member of his firm. There was a strong hint that 'firm' meant a criminal firm. Unbeknown to Liz, the plan was to entice Jimmy Fulton to the mainland with some things he would likely want: a driving job with a dodgy outfit; a chance to make money; to distance himself from possible execution which was likely if he stayed in Belfast; to become closer to Muriel Gibson, a trusted LVF member. The RUC's Special Branch (SB) gave Fulton a full Osman warning[12] to reinforce the same message issued to him on his arrival at Heathrow following his deportation from the United States.

---

[12] It is a warning of a death threat or risk of murder, issued by the British police or authorities to the prospective victim. It comes from the 1998 legal case of Osman vs United Kingdom which was heard by the European Court of Human Rights.

After a couple of weeks, Muriel picked up the keys to her lovely new house in Camborne and began turning it into a home. She loved her neighbours – Dave and his lady, Sam. They were so helpful and friendly. So, a friendship began to develop. Dave and Sam had a market stall selling baby stuff: second-hand push chairs, baby clothes, highchairs, baby baths and the like. On one occasion, Sam took ill, leaving Dave needing a hand on the stall, so he asked Muriel if she could help for a few bob to be paid cash in hand. Muriel jumped at the chance and seemed grateful for the opportunity. Dave used a long wheel Transit van for the market business. It also came in handy when Muriel needed any large items moving that she'd bought locally from charity shops to furnish her new house. Dave and Sam also had a small lock-up garage that Muriel visited when she helped on the market stall. She would go there with Sam or Dave to help load and unload the Transit. It was no accident that she noticed cases of booze, wine, spirits and fags stashed in the back. Dave and Sam obviously had a side-line in cheap fags and booze, Muriel must have thought, and that was the object of the deception. Muriel's contact with Jimmy was now daily and it was clear from the probe and phone taps that he was seriously looking at coming across to spend some time with her. Time for the Op Team to turn the screw on Muriel and Jimmy via Liz.

So, the stage was now set for Jimmy. Muriel was settled into her house in Camborne. Dave and Sam had befriended her and won over her trust. Jimmy had been kicked out of the USA. Neil was set up back in Plymouth needing and looking for a good, trusted, loyal driver to join his team. Muriel had been picked up on the probe and phone taps talking to Jimmy who was now back in Portadown but believed he was not safe in Northern Ireland.

"Get yourself over here, Jim. There's a job here and you can get your head down with me until you and Tanya get sorted out. I've been telling my mate Liz that you're a top fella and she's mentioned it to her man, Neil. The word is that it is not safe for you back home," was the gist of Muriel's communications with her long-time friend Jim Fulton.

In March 2000, Fulton arrived in Camborne. The final piece of the jigsaw had just walked into place under his own free will. It was an amazing bit of police work, but now even more extraordinary police action was to follow. It was as if Jimmy Fulton had walked onto the set of *The Truman Show*. Welcome, Jimmy! Welcome to a world created and populated by Colin Port and his team of dedicated covert officers.

Muriel called Liz in a state of excitement. "Hi, Liz, yer man's here. He arrived last night. Is Neil still looking for a driver?"

The day after the call to Liz, the UCO known as Neil drove his car down to Camborne with Liz as his passenger to meet Jimmy. He dropped Liz off at Muriel's house and he and Jimmy went out for a drive and a chat. After about five minutes, Neil pulled over and said, "Right, let's see how you drive, son. Swap places." Jimmy took control of the black Lexus with tinted windows and drove round for half an hour with Neil giving him directions. Jimmy seemed a little nervous – not surprising as he thought this was a driving test. If he failed, no job. *Nothing to get nervous about, Jimmy, son*, thought Neil, the *fucking job's yours. It's a done deal, you're on the books.*

William James Fulton was now the property of Operation George. The first stages of the plan had succeeded; a plan first devised whilst Fulton was in custody in the USA for firearms and drugs offences. It was a cunning, audacious and exceptional plan, expertly executed under the supervision of Colin Port together with assistance from the FBI and the British government, to ensure that Jimmy was extradited from the USA and returned to the United Kingdom. Colin Port needed Jimmy on the mainland. Now he was.

# CHAPTER 12

## Neil

After the Cornwall undercover team had whispered words in Muriel Gibson's ear, Neil was one of the first Plymouth-based UCOs to engage with Jim Fulton. Neil had an air of authority and a panache which easily lent themselves to his role as the crime lord of the Plymouth organised crime group – the firm. It was a role he carried off to perfection and it wasn't long before Jimmy Fulton was shooting off his mouth to ingratiate himself with Neil, the boss, following his recruitment into the Plymouth firm. Initially, Neil engaged Fulton in conversation over breakfast in Plymouth's Port

O' Call café, talking to him about family matters once Fulton had mentioned names. Neil was then able to ask about Jim's wife, Tanya, his brother Mark's release from prison on parole, and could query the possibility of Jim recruiting a friend, Phillip McLean, into the firm. They were normal friendly conversations and extended to Neil inquiring about Mark's children and Muriel Gibson's family in California. These conversations were all based on facts freely offered by both Gibson and Fulton so Neil was safe in discussing these matters.

After breakfast, Jim drove Neil to London after Neil had told him he needed to collect some money. That gave Neil most of the rest of the day to hear what Fulton had to say on the journey out and back. Jim carried on talking about family, including Gary Fulton's sister who was married to an RUC police officer. But later, and possibly prompted by the mention of the RUC, Jim started talking about Drumcree when Swinger (Mark Fulton), his brother, was in jail. He explained about the huge security presence because of the events of the previous year and his assurance to the 'Orangemen' he wouldn't bring any weapons to the protests.

Jim said, "They got their faces reddened the year before when we got the machine guns and all out like."

Then there was more chat about Drumcree, Northern Ireland and about Billy Wright and his finances. Wright was the former leader of the LVF but now deceased. After a long period of quiet Fulton said, "One time, Swinger, Billy and Tony and Jamesy went out and stiffed the Boyle brothers, two of them, both Provies… fucking just out the other side of Lurgan. And they stiffed them that quick… got back in the car.

The weapons were taken away, but they were still covered for you know forensics. They drove into Lurgan … but into a check point. And Billy says 'right everybody act drunk.' And you know they hadn't even, they hadn't got word about the shooting. They'd had no reports come in."

"Oh, right," Neil said. It was important for him to seem only half interested, when in reality he knew he was potentially recording crucial detail about a murder.

Neil's frequent trips to the bank with Jimmy driving would involve the round trip from Plymouth to London. Owing to previous visits, Jimmy knew it was a private bank in Mayfair. Neil told him he had a safety deposit box there and he often mentioned Stuart, the first name of his personal banking manager. It was often the case, after the visit to the bank, that Neil told Jimmy the next stop was a business meeting in the Ritz Hotel with an associate and friend who was stopping off in London for a few days before flying back to his mountain villa high in the Canadian Rockies.

Neil was a master at creating these intriguing scenes for Jimmy to imagine, using simple suggestions and veiled speech. Jimmy revelled in the kudos that came with having a boss who moved in such exciting circles, visiting high-flying associates in world-famous venues like the Ritz in Mayfair. Neil would sometimes carry a package or briefcase into the bank, making sure to mix it up. Jimmy would always drop his 'boss' directly outside the bank and drive off and wait in a residential street just off the main road. To keep things looking real, Neil did have a deposit box inside the bank so he could go into the building and gain access to the box. He'd place the package or the contents of the briefcase into his box or depart with a package that he had placed there a few days before without Jimmy's involvement or knowledge. Neil would wrap the package to suggest it was a bundle of bank notes by its size and shape. He would take advantage of this time alone to put a fresh tape into his recording device ready for the next two-hour session with Jimmy.

On leaving the Mayfair bank, Jimmy would drive to Neil's lunch appointment at the Ritz Hotel. Jimmy would drop Neil outside the hotel and drive off. Walking into the hotel reception area, Neil would wait for a call to say Jimmy had cleared the plot. Neil now knew it was safe to leave the hotel without being spotted by Jimmy. Forever the professional, Neil had a cover story ready for any staff member who might ask if they could help. "No thanks, it's okay. I'm just waiting for my colleague to join me; he'll be here in a minute. Thanks."

Within seconds, Neil's phone would ring and he would get a cryptic message from his Cover Officer that Jimmy was away. Neil would reply in an equally enigmatic message that suggested to anyone who may overhear him that he understood and would meet him there [a pre-arranged location] in a minute or two. Neil would leave the hotel without disturbing the environment or attracting suspicion and make his way the short distance to the agreed meeting location with his Cover Officer. On arrival, Neil would go to the toilet to deactivate his recording device before talking to the Cover Officer. These locations weren't the Ritz, but the coffee and pizza were delicious and courtesy of Colin Port. When deemed appropriate, Neil would reactivate his device and put a call into

Jimmy and ask him to pick him up. "Okay, Jimmy, fed and watered. Come and pick me up please. I'll be on the pavement on the opposite side of the road across from the hotel."

"No problem boss, I'll be there in two," Jimmy would reply.

Jimmy was in his element. He would often tell the other UCOs over a few beers how he enjoyed playing cat and mouse with who he called the "Stasi" (London traffic wardens). He told them how he would sit on a parking meter without paying with a view of the street and pavements looking out for the Stasi. He said it reminded him of 'operations' in Ireland and if he could operate on the streets of Northern Ireland and not get nicked, an over enthusiastic traffic warden pounding the streets of London wasn't going to worry him. As soon as Jimmy saw the warden approaching, he'd drive off round the block to where he thought the warden had come from, then park again. Jimmy's rationale was that the guy had a route; a set pattern of patrolling his patch like a soldier and therefore would not be back in Jimmy's new location for some time.

Jimmy would delight in saying, "You boys want to take a few lessons from the master of trickery." The UCOs present would smile inwardly at Jimmy's words, safe in the knowledge that only they understood the irony. To foster his grand deception, Neil told Fulton he had a flat in London, as well as his place in Plymouth. He also mentioned stocks and shares to Fulton, letting the target think he was a wealthy and successful crime boss. This was reinforced by hints of other dubious activities. He also hinted he was a millionaire, throwing in mention of a portfolio of properties in Spain and

Portugal, but in a quite a casual way. The understatement was deliberate. Neil wished to give the impression that he was successful because he and his firm stayed off the law enforcement radar. He said nothing to dissuade Fulton that it was he who had financed the purchase of a Renault Laguna for Jim's sole use. The arrangements were made for Fulton to be paid for his new driving job for the 'firm.' Later, Fulton called his mum in Northern Island and the conversation was recorded as he talked proudly about his new job, leaving out all the dodgy bits. He also told his mother he was being paid £2,500 every fortnight.

Neil later commented, "He probably wanted his mum to think that he had a proper job, and he wasn't involved in anything else." The rest of the UCOs thought the same.

Fulton was paid by the firm for his work as a driver over a period of sixty-four weeks. He received an average weekly wage of £455.27, or £1,821.06 a month. The payments varied in date and amount depending on the work Fulton had done. For example, in one five-week period no payments at all were made to Fulton for wages, but on some occasions large amounts were paid: in July 2000 and April 2001 he received £1,000; in March 2001, £900, and another £570 in April 2001, plus £500 in December 2000. On top of his wages, Fulton also benefited from the generosity of the undercover officers, who paid for meals and refreshments. Once more, human nature plays its part in Fulton trying to advance himself in the hierarchy of the firm. He thought he was on to a good thing.

# CHAPTER 13

## First Meeting

Just like actors on stage and screen, UCOs need a rest occasionally. But a key difference is that UCOs are paid as usual even when not 'working', as opposed to actors using the euphemism of 'resting' to disguise the fact they are temporarily unemployed.

A UCO with the alias Robbie was sitting at his desk when his legend mobile phone rang.

"Do you fancy a bit of work?"

It was the boss in London. The boss, a senior investigating officer (SIO) met Robbie in London and briefed him to deliver a car to Plymouth where he would meet another UCO and the target of the operation – Jim Fulton. At that stage it was supposed to be a quick in and out job. Deliver the car and that's it. When Robbie got to Plymouth, driving there in his own car,[13] he had another briefing where he was told the operation was top secret and nothing about it could be disclosed. He was also told never to mention a thing about his military background. Before the briefing was over, the briefing officer, glancing at some notes, said, "And not a thing about being a Catholic." Robbie, feeling a little perplexed initially, soon came to realise the vital importance of those instructions.

Robbie then returned to London to collect the car that was to be delivered to Fulton – a Renault Laguna – and drove it to Plymouth. As per his instructions, he headed to a pub where he was to meet another UCO – Neil – and

---

[13] Notionally 'his car' but owned by the police authority and used by Robbie as 'his car.'

Fulton. Robbie already knew Neil from other operations and, as part of the usual steps, had called him while on his way to Plymouth to firm up arrangements for the meet. Robbie met up with Neil and Fulton inside the pub. Neil, making out he was someone 'big' in the firm, told Robbie to hand over the car keys to Fulton. All went well until Neil pulled Robbie over, out of Fulton's sight and hearing, and told him he was feeling ill. "I mean ill… really ill… genuinely ill. I'm going to have to go back to the flat. Will you be okay?"

"I'll be fine," Robbie said. "No problem."

Robbie and Jim whiled away the hours, chatting away like 'new best friends,' and that was the start of almost two years Robbie spent in the company of Jim Fulton, a relationship Fulton never realised was a fabrication. After Robbie slept overnight in the Plymouth flat, a safe house, he met up with Jim again the following morning by mutual arrangement and sanctioned by a Plymouth Cover Officer.

They strolled through a trailer park near the docks close to a freight terminal when Jim started to talk, entirely unprompted, about his days in Belfast. He told Robbie about his bomb maker. Jim said, "He's good. He can make a bomb so wee it fits inside a cigarette packet." After that, Fulton went his separate way, using the car Robbie had delivered as his wheels. Fulton was unaware that car had been doctored, lumped up – kitted out with listening devices and an immobiliser.

Following the usual routine, Robbie went to meet a Cover Officer for a debrief. It was at that Plymouth debriefing where he met Neil, a UCO who played a major role in the operation. Neil played the part of the boss of the crime gang and explained to Robbie that the objective was to gain Fulton's confidence by recruiting him into the Plymouth-based organised crime group, initially as a driver. Hence the reason for the Renault Laguna that Robbie had driven down from London.

During the debrief, Robbie relayed what had happened with Fulton, which was all recorded, and whilst Robbie was making his own notes in his pocket notebook, one of the team said, "Do you think you can hang around for a few days?"

"Yeah, I'm sure I can," Robbie said. That was the start of Robbie's long so-called friendship with Jimmy Fulton. Neil, Robbie and the rest of the UCOs came to address Fulton as 'Jimmy' rather than a more formal 'Jim' as they got on friendly terms.

# CHAPTER 14

## Robbie a Fixture

Now Robbie was a fixture on the team, plans were laid as to how best to control Jimmy Fulton in the hope he might say something about the Rosemary Nelson murder. That was the prime objective. From Colin Port downwards, the whole Operation George team was conscious Fulton was a ruthless terrorist, and accordingly it was vital he did not engage in any terrorist activities on the English mainland, or elsewhere for that matter. It is somewhat otiose to consider the implications if he were to explode a bomb in England whilst part of the Plymouth 'firm.'

Neil, Dave, Robbie and one other were to become the nucleus of the UCOs 'palling up' to Fulton. It was they, together with the Cover Officers, who discussed the various scams or subterfuges designed to bring Fulton closer to the 'firm' and thus increasing the opportunities for the target to talk freely. All these conversations were to be recorded using gadgets hidden on the UCOs, secreted in vehicles, and later using probes hidden in the homes of both Fulton and Muriel Gibson in Cornwall.

The Cover Officers would rotate from time to time, but one of them would always be close by and staying in an hotel. The deceptions were freely discussed between all present; sometimes a Cover Officer would float an idea or more often the scams were thought up by one of the UCOs. Robbie's legend was partly built on a background of the haulage industry and Robbie had a valid HGV 1 licence. To be precise, there were two. One in his real name and one in an alias for undercover work. This was ripe for introducing Fulton to a world of high value thefts of lorry trailers and their cargo. Trailers loaded with booze, cigarettes, or computer parts were the favourites, but one or another of the team would throw in an idea based on real jobs they had worked on in the past.

Once an idea had been adopted, the UCOs and Cover Officers would approach the Operational Team to discuss the logistics: the 'what, where and how' of the scam. The Operational Team would then locate and obtain the resources, whether they be radios, lorry loads of booze or fags, and on other future scams an armoured car and a priceless work of art. These deceptions were vital if they were to control Jimmy Fulton. That control was a given. They needed him in their company as much as possible to allow him to talk, which was all recorded.

It wasn't always a planned staged theft. Sometimes he would be invited to drive them to different places all over England. In a typical job, he would drive one or more of the UCOs to London. He'd drop them off and the UCO or UCOs would disappear, telling him they were going to an important meeting. The way it was said was designed to let him believe it was something dodgy. He would wait in the car thinking, *I've landed on my feet here with this gang.* On occasions he would drop one of the UCOs off at a bank, usually Neil because he had a safety deposit box there. That was designed to make him think they were real big-time players in the criminal underworld.

These subterfuges were gradually ratcheted up so sometimes Jimmy would be told to come inside to the meeting but to stay in the corner to keep an eye on the parked car or 'Old Bill.' The meeting was all pre-arranged so one of the UCOs would be meeting up with another UCO, not part of the operation but playing a minor but important role in the grand deception. The two UCOs would sit and talk about anything, but out of earshot of Jimmy. Once the meeting was over, Jimmy would drive back to Plymouth with the UCO and talk all the way. These subterfuges were all sanctioned, recorded in writing and authorised by the boss. It was then the logistical support kicked in, supplying whatever was required for any one scam. Although the UCOs knew this operation was deadly serious, they did have fun coming up with the ideas for the scams. Some were actioned and others put on the back burner. But all had the same intention: to keep Jimmy Fulton thinking he was running with a firm of serious proportions.

# CHAPTER 15

## Slough

"I need you to do a bit of work with Robbie for a few days. You okay with that, Jimmy?' Neil asked.

"I'm yer man," Jimmy replied, all too keen to impress Neil, and he was now on the payroll of the Plymouth gang.

"Okay then. Meet him at the Port O' Call at eight tomorrow morning," Neil instructed.

Plymouth's Port O' Call café was near to the Hoe and a regular meeting spot for Jimmy and the UCOs. It served what some call a 'big boys' or 'fat boys' breakfast. Others call that huge cholesterol laden English breakfast by other names, one of which is amusing and often used in Sheffield – 'the full train smash.' Over breakfast, Robbie said, "Right, we're going to have a drive up to Slough. There're loads of industrial estates there and we need to have a mooch around and check out a trailer worth nicking. I'm told there is, but I need to see with my own eyes."

"Right yer are, Robbie," Jimmy said, delighted to be placed in a position of trust within the firm. It was mission accomplished in that Robbie and Jimmy would be spending five hours or more together in the confines of a car wired for sound, as was Robbie. The people who'd listen to those tapes were located many miles from Plymouth and buried away in a police headquarters back office. They would listen after the event and make notes before passing the tapes on to the transcribers. Those transcripts were typed documents and, in the future, would be used as evidential material in the case against Fulton and Gibson.

In one revealing moment during that recording, Jimmy laughed about when he'd invite people round to tea. He went on to explain that in his world back in Northern Ireland getting invited around for your tea means you're going to get punished – a shooting or kneecapping. He did so with a laugh and a smile in his eyes. Robbie stayed calm… and silent. Fulton went on to demonstrate to Robbie how he'd kneecap somebody. If it were somebody he liked, he'd put it through the fleshy bit of the thigh, close to the knee. If it were somebody that he didn't like and deserved the worst he could possibly get, he'd put the bullet through his kneecap and cripple them for life. All through this, Fulton laughed and joked and suddenly switched to how he had grown up in Belfast. Robbie gained the impression Fulton wasn't a soldier. He wouldn't have gone gun to gun – mano a mano. But Robbie remained silent, keeping his innermost thoughts private.

With every recording it felt like they were getting closer to snaring Jimmy Fulton, but he still hadn't mentioned the Rosemary Nelson murder. After some consultation the team decided to up the stakes. In three weeks they would stage a lorry theft. By upping the stakes like that, they could convince Jimmy how serious they were. The question remained: would he finally give them what they needed, or would everything unravel before they got their man?

# CHAPTER 16

## Cash in Transit

The team more and more enjoyed the surreal nature of the deceptions and revelled in the private references to the *Truman Show*. They decided to give Jim bigger parts to play to make him feel even more part of the 'gang.' Someone came up with the idea of staging a cash in transit robbery. It was a risk, bearing in mind it would possibly involve violence which was Jim's bread and butter.

The plan went ahead with Robbie and Jimmy driving to a hotel in the home counties. The idea was for them to meet up with Neil and other members of a crime gang that Robbie and Neil had previously worked with. The other players were, of course, UCOs who all knew each other well. The main player on their side was a guy called Bobby. At the meeting in a hotel bedroom with Jimmy present, Bobby started telling Robbie and Neil about a job he was planning, but he needed some extra bodies with certain talents to pull it off. There were about five men in the room when Bobby unveiled the plan for this job.

Completely off the cuff, Robbie started digging and asking questions about details. Bobby and Neil knew to play along even when things got a bit heated.

"I hear you but I gotta know, whose bit of work is this?" asked Robbie.

"Can't tell you that," Bobby said.

"Well, okay, who will be on the pavement at the time of the race [the planned event]? You're talking millions in cash so there's a good chance armed cops would be close. I need to know the head honcho will be there with me, so I know it won't turn to shit," Robbie said, almost shouting. It was getting heated and turned up a few notches by Bobby and Robbie yelling and stabbing the air every time they were making a point. Neil gave Robbie a certain look which was code for enough. The scene was now set. The meeting broke up and Robbie and Jimmy went for a pint in the hotel lounge. Bugsy, one of Bobby's gang (in reality another UCO), joined them.

"What the fuck's up with your boss?" Robbie said.

"Ah, don't worry about it. He's okay. No problem," Bugsy said.

After finishing their drinks, Jimmy and Robbie drove back to Plymouth, some four hours away.

Fulton talked about this job incessantly and said, "Right up my street. Guns, violence and money." He seemed upset about the argument back in the hotel room.

"Forget it," Robbie said.

"Don't you worry, Robbie. I'll dig two holes, one for the money and one for that cunt Bobby. No one talks to you like that in front of me and gets away with it," Fulton said.

Later that night at a debriefing session, Robbie was finally able to laugh at what had happened, especially Jim Fulton's 'two holes' comment. Unable to resist a bit of leg-pulling, Robbie saw his old mate Bobby and said, "You're a dead man walking."

It was then back to serious work. The team needed to plan the staged cash in transit job. As always it was a case of keeping Jimmy occupied and under control so they would go and recon the plot. This gave them ample time with Jimmy travelling to London and capturing his admissions on tape. The first stage of planning involved the Operational Team and Cover Officers obtaining an armoured car and access to a disused secure bonded warehouse somewhere in East London. A UCO from outside the team was briefed to drive the armoured car.

The Plymouth team had arranged for the Cover Officer to get hold of some walkie-talkies for the scam. True to form, the Metropolitan Police Service (MPS) Cover Officer went out and purchased the best, all singing and dancing two-way handheld walkie-talkies. They were complicated to the uninitiated, with a complex array of switches, buttons and dials.

 As one forthright UCO exclaimed on first testing one of the radios, "For fuck's sake mate, is this kit supplied by NASA? You could hold a conversation with someone stood on Mars with these things. They must have cost thousands. The only problem is you need a PhD in electronics to switch the fucking thing on."

Following the plan, Robbie and Jim set off from Plymouth to London on another exciting day of murderous conversation between them. Robbie's ploy to make sure the recordings were clear was turning off the in-car radio when he got in. Covering his real motive, he said, "I don't like that shit that comes across the airways." It was reputed Robbie loved his music and prided himself as a pop aficionado, sometimes telling anyone who would care to listen that popular music was his thing in any pub quiz round. So now pop music was added to the list he couldn't disclose in his legend, along with the truths he was once a soldier and is a Roman Catholic, albeit of the lapsed kind.

At some point on the journey, Robbie, who was in the passenger seat, retrieved the walkie-talkies from a bag on the back seat. He examined the mass of dials and switches, trying to figure out how to turn them on. Pressing some buttons, Robbie was horrified to hear the car radio clicking as if in weird electronic duet with the walkie-talkie. Panic set in. Robbie's thoughts were filled with expletives, and he could sense a cold sweat running down his back. He suddenly realised the car radio and the walkie-talkie were on the same wavelength. Worried that Jimmy would become suspicious, and desperately concerned that the whole operation was about to go tits-up, he managed to shrug the whole thing off in front of Jimmy.

Sometime later, they arrive at the disused bonded warehouse in East London and met up with another UCO called Hands (on account of having hands the size of large shovels). Robbie gave Hands one of the walkie-talkies and a quick lesson on how it worked, though Hands seemed a little distracted. Robbie conducted a test call, deliberately avoiding using any recognised voice procedure or knowledge of how you should talk over a radio with words like 'over' or 'out.' He spoke as if he was talking to him face to face. Jimmy interrupted and started to say things like, "Press the PTT button, Robbie." He was eager to help in any way he could, undoubtedly thinking of all those millions. Robbie knew from his former military life that PTT was short for 'Press to Talk' or 'Press to Transmit.' It was clear to Robbie his feigned ineptness in radio management, voice procedures and protocols were both amusing to Jimmy and frustrated him, to the point where Jimmy said, "Robbie, you drive, and I'll do the fucking radio." Robbie did just that, jumping into the driving seat and letting Jimmy take over the radio. Robbie was impressed with Jimmy's expertise as he listened to him using phrases like "Hello one. This is zero, over," and "Standby, standby one. There is movement at the premises."

A friendly insider at the warehouse had told the team what time to expect the armoured car to exit. At the precise time, out came the money truck. Robbie and Jimmy noted the time and the direction of travel, knowing Hands was in position a bit further away as a second pair of eyes as part of the staged recon for the job itself. Once they had seen what they needed, Robbie and Jimmy called up Hands so he could make his way over to them. They had a brief conversation where there was a load of piss taking at Robbie's expense about his radio techniques. Then Hands walked away, with Robbie still in the driving seat. Robbie soon realised Hands' walkie-talkie was on open mic, but still in his pocket. If Hands was to call his Cover Officer to update them on what had just happened, the conversation would come through the walkie-talkie, and the entire operation would be blown. Jimmy still had the walkie-talkie so Robbie couldn't turn it off. Trying not to panic, Robbie's brain went into warp speed to come up with a plan.

Robbie could see Hands and was dreading him taking his phone out. Robbie's first thought was to drive at him and knock him over if he reached for his phone. He would try to avoid causing him serious injury, just wing him a bit, anything to stop him reaching for and using his phone. Lucky for Hands, Robbie had a second thought.... he rang him. Robbie managed to indicate cryptically what the problem was. After some initial confusion on the part of Hands, he twigged what Robbie was saying, reached into his pocket and turned the walkie-talkie off. Though they were able to laugh about it in the debrief that followed, Robbie had been so close to the operation collapsing that he must have had nightmares about it. Jimmy had talked about his previous violence. Who knows what he might have done in that van when he realised how he'd been hoodwinked.

# CHAPTER 17

## The Reversing Lorry

The cash-in-transit job was eventually abandoned, but not until several dry runs following the armoured car with Jimmy for company in the wired-for-sound car. That provided many hours for Jimmy to talk, and he did talk. In addition to following the armoured car, UCOs and Jimmy scoped various likely places to ambush the truck. Most of them were in the New Forest, a popular tourist area, which was a factor in calling off the plan – along with complications around having to use real weapons to make it all look genuine. Every one of the team, never mind the bosses in Belfast and London, knew this was a big no-no as far as Jim Fulton's involvement was concerned. The team deflected Jimmy's interest into helping steal a high-value load of cigarettes instead. Over one million quid's worth to be exact. The load 'belonged' to a government agency and for them to play ball, Colin Port had to hastily arrange for the entire load to be underwritten to the tune of £1.2 million, now just over £2 million in today's money, which included the vast amount of taxation due on the cigarettes. Daniel Defoe was correct when he wrote in *The Political History of the Devil*, in 1726: "Things as certain as death and taxes, can be more firmly believ'd." H.M. Government was prepared to 'lose' the goods but not the taxes.

Robbie was the UCO with a licence to drive big lorries and he set off to a bonded warehouse near to the docks in Dover, Kent, to collect the load in a forty-foot long, nondescript curtain-side trailer. Spare a thought for Robbie right now. Can you imagine a non-ranking detective signing for and being responsible for £1.2 million worth of product? If this had been a drug deal or some other sort of undercover operation with a parcel of that value on the pavement the boss would have had a fully armed surveillance team with eyes on that the parcel 24/7. Some UCOs have done jobs with much less money on the plot and there were more guns deployed than they had at the Alamo.

In the real world, loads of this value would have tracker devices buried in the trailer or load. Robbie's experience was invaluable. Some of that was from other undercover work and some gleaned from real haulage industry experience. He knew how to combat any challenge Jimmy might come up with because he would say they had a man on the inside of the knock-off. He would explain the guy had reassured him that any tracker had been sabotaged. Jimmy never asked. The easiest question to answer is the question that is never asked, but he was ready if asked.

Setting up all these staged jobs would involve casing the locations, planning routes, working out time and distance, arranging access to a 'slaughter' (criminal slang for warehouse) where the parcel would be broken up ready for distribution to trusted buyers. All this gave the time for the UCOs to be with Jimmy for hours on end or a one to one where all sorts of conversations took place.

Robbie did a few recons with Jimmy on the cigarettes theft just to spend time with him and generate conversation. Eventually, Robbie did the job of hitching up the tractor unit to the trailer with Jimmy acting as his third eye. Robbie smoothly had the trailer away and set off for the slaughter. Jimmy was following in the Laguna with both men in contact using mobile phones. Robbie instructed Jimmy to drive ahead to a choke point to check if anything was following the lorry. Once Jimmy gave Robbie an all clear, Robbie told Jimmy to follow at a distance to monitor any vehicles that were in convoy with the lorry. He got Jimmy to carry out anti and counter surveillance.

"This is the dog's bollocks," Jimmy said over the phone. He was loving it, thinking he was back operating in Northern Ireland. Robbie, sat in the cab of the truck, couldn't resist a wry smile. He knew these antics gave the Plymouth firm a professional aura and credibility. *But there's still a lot that could go* wrong, he reminded himself.

Robbie and Jimmy arrived at the warehouse, which had all been arranged by the Plymouth cover team beforehand. The team had always wanted Jimmy to feel he was working his way up the ranks of the firm and gaining their respect and trust. This was paying dividends. Unbeknownst to Jimmy, prior to arriving at the warehouse the technical team had worked their magic for sound, after which they had handed over the warehouse keys to the UCOs. A Cover Officer would give a crash course, showing how to activate the sound and the best locations for best quality recordings. What nobody could change was the physical layout of the industrial estate where the warehouse was located. It was best suited to large Ford Transit vans and not forty-foot trailers. The access roads were cramped and ram full of delivery vans during daylight hours. Not the best scenario for backing in a forty-foot trailer into a warehouse never designed to accommodate large trucks. Together, Robbie and Jimmy had visited the 'slaughter' a few times before the day of the race [the event] to familiarise themselves with the location, locks, light switches, door operation and stuff like that. These trips again generated opportunities to spend time with and occupying Jimmy. That was the name of the game in their world.

Robbie soon realised a forklift truck and a pallet truck were needed. The pallet truck proved easy for the cover team and was sourced locally. Robbie had no idea where it had come from. Cover Officers from the cover team put it inside the warehouse until needed.

*That part is now sorted, but what about the forklift truck?* Robbie thought. After all, there was no way they could handball forty feet of fags off a trailer. One of the team found a plant hire place on the estate that rented out forklift trucks and other plant out by the day. Robbie was the only UCO on the team who had a licence to drive a forklift truck, so it fell on him to arrange the hire. No problem, as he had all the necessary covert documentation to produce to the guy in the hire centre: a driving licence, a separate forklift licence, proof of address and most importantly to the hire guy, bank details for the hire payment.

Robbie arranged to collect the truck the following day without Jimmy being there, as the plan was to meet Hands to run the plans by him to ensure all went like clockwork. On arriving at the warehouse, Robbie spotted Hands' car parked up but no sign of his colleague anywhere. Robbie later told the team, "I'm the only person with keys to the warehouse so I know he's not playing one of his stupid games of hiding inside from me ready to jump out to scare the shit out of me. I know the tea van round the corner does a nice brew and bacon butty, so I head off round there thinking that's where he'll be. As I'm making my way round to the van what do I see?"

Robbie continued to describe Hands driving towards him in the forklift truck, right down the middle of the road. He was holding up a line of traffic that couldn't pass because of his road position. Robbie added, "He was smiling from ear to ear and shouted out to me, 'A piece of piss this mate, don't know what all the drama is about who can drive what.'" Hands had told Robbie as he was on the plot early, he'd go and pick up the forklift. He informed the hire guy that he worked for Robbie and he'd sent him to pick up the truck.

"Convincing people to believe us is part of being a UCO, I guess," added Robbie at the end of telling the tale to the assembled team.

And so the scene was set. The team had the warehouse, the listening device, a forklift, the lorry, the trailer and the cherry on the cake: a load of fags to the value of £1.2 million.

At around 2:00 am Robbie called Hands on the mobile and told him he was five minutes out and to get ready. Five minutes later, Robbie pulled into the industrial estate and positioned the lorry so he could reverse around the corner of the building line and come to a halt alongside the warehouse shutter door. As he braked to a halt with that unmistakeable hiss of air brakes, Jimmy, with the keys in hand, was off like a dog with a bone to open the door and switch on the lights and, unbeknownst to him, the listening devices planted in the warehouse.

Robbie started the tricky manoeuvre of reversing and turning the trailer at the same time. It was a tight fit but doable. Hands was on foot, keeping pace with the trailer from behind, helping to guide Robbie round the corner and into the best position by the shutter door. The trailer started coming round like a dream. Hands was doing a great job, shouting out, "Keep coming, keep coming, a bit of left hand down." Then, as Robbie later put it, "My eyeline clears the side of the building line and my retinas are destroyed by a brilliant white light. I can't see a fucking thing."

Hands continued to shout, "Keep coming mate, keep it on that, keep coming."

Luckily, Robbie sussed out what was going on. He looked up at the source of the bright lights, shielding his eyes, and could just make out that Hands had parked his car at the top of the yard with the headlights on main beam, no doubt trying to help.

Later, Robbie continued his story, "All he's done is blind me... bloody hell, Hands! I try to get his attention by shouting, 'Hands, mate, I can't see fuck all, switch the fucking lights off.'

"Hands continues to shout out, 'Come on, keep coming, keep coming.'

"I'm shouting 'Hands, Hands, switch the fucking lights off, I can't see.'

"All I heard was Hands, 'Keep coming, keep coming.'

"Over the noise of the truck and Hands calling out I can't hear a word. Out of frustration I shout out Hands' real nickname, 'Lucky, shut the fuck up and switch those fucking lights off.' That did the trick, as Hands stopped shouting. I could see his silhouette in the wing mirror walking towards me along the side of the trailer.

"He stopped by the driver's door and looked up at me with wide eyes and said, 'You've just called me by my nickname.'

"'Yeah, I know mate, but you weren't responding to Hands.'

"'You've just called me Lucky on the tape,' he said.

"'Yeah mate, and you've just done it now,' I said.

"'Fucking hell that's shit,' he said.

"So, I said, 'Yeah, I'm sorry mate, but do me a favour, switch the fucking headlights off. You're blinding me. I can't see shit.'"

At the official debriefing the team heard how Hands complied with Robbie's request and deftly manoeuvred the trailer into A1 position. It was confirmed that Jimmy had been in the warehouse and heard and saw nothing. Robbie had jumped down from the cab to where Hands was standing as Jimmy opened the barn doors at the rear of the trailer. Robbie then went into the warehouse and within seconds reappeared driving the forklift. Jimmy stayed in the warehouse, directing where to drop each pallet according to brand. He oversaw handing over the booty to the buyers throughout the next twenty-four hours. Robbie lifted the first two pallets off and into the warehouse and then started moving pallets to the rear of the trailer, using the hand-operated pallet where his now ex mate Hands was waiting to use the big forklift truck. The job went like clockwork, and they unloaded the fags in record time. Jimmy's job now was to stay there and slaughter the load to numerous vans and small lorries that would be arriving over the next hours. Every van and lorry were driven by a motley crew of UCOs all drafted in solely for this scam. Hands and Robbie left Jimmy in charge. Hands set off in his car with Robbie leaving in the lorry to dump the empty trailer. But not before Robbie dissuaded Jimmy from his plan to torch the trailer.

Jimmy was relieved sometime later by Hands so Jimmy could go home and get some sleep. Once Jimmy was indoors and a suitable time allowed for him to drop off, the operation in reverse had to take place. The load had to go back. Jimmy was monitored by the technical people using the probes and once he seemed to be in dreamland after a successful job, the same fleet of vans and lorries returned all the fags to the warehouse. The building and its valuable contents were secured, and someone stayed there until the area around the warehouse had fallen silent again. That was Robbie's cue to return with the tractor unit and trailer to reload and return the goods to the rightful owner.

During the operation debriefing, Hands was heard to demand, "That part of the tape needs PII cos dickhead Robbie called me by my nickname."

Robbie said immediately, "Sorry, Lucky, no harm done mate."

One further point was up for discussion at the debriefing when someone asked, "Did anyone else see the real police in that marked police car?"

"No, we were too busy unloading over a million quid's worth of fags," said a voice at the back of the room.

"Lazy bastards, three in the morning and they can't be arsed to ask us what we're doing," said another.

# CHAPTER 18

## Work of Art

As always, a new scam was conceived at a joint meeting of the UCOs, with the cover team sitting down and dreaming up a 'bit of work' that they could run out over a prolonged period. They also kept the prime objective in mind: to spend time with Jimmy to occupy him and let him talk about his life in Northern Ireland 'fighting the fight.' They had to create scenarios that would genuinely play out over several deployments and structure them in a criminal way. They knew each bit of work had to be milked for everything they could get out of it.

This was how the 'stolen and priceless work of art' scam was invented.

The possibility of a 'big earner' was casually floated around by the UCOs in Jimmy's company, so he had some idea that a big job was in the making and come the time the firm would sit down and discuss it. Those talks would involve Jimmy too. The germ of an idea had taken hold in Jimmy's mind, so much so, on a full day road trip with Robbie, he said, "Has Neil mentioned anything to you about a big job coming off?"

Robbie played dumb. Jimmy, hardly able to conceal his excitement, continued, "For fuck's sake, Robbie, don't let on I've mentioned it but it's to do with a fucking expensive painting."

The scam was in play. They had created a scenario for Jimmy, and he was walking wide eyed into it. Sometime later, Neil called the meeting. Neil, Dave, Robbie and Jimmy attended when Neil laid out the plan. Robbie at that point looked across at Jimmy who wore a 'told you so' smile. Neil made it clear they were going to have a fat pay day for doing next to nothing but with a bit of risk around it. He explained that he was middling the sale of a stolen, priceless work of art, and had an overseas buyer for the painting.

"Our buyer is the front. I happen to know he's working for a Belgian firm but as far as anyone is concerned, I'm doing business with only the buyer, the front man. Likewise, the real seller is known to no one," Neil said, deliberately sounding mysterious as to who had possession and control of the painting at this time. He added that "the market for works of art is a mystery to me but none of us need know anything about it or who the real buyer and seller is. That's where we come in with the Belgian outfit, to keep the real identities of the parties a closely guarded secret. That's how it works."

Neil carried on laying out the next steps which were to meet up and have preliminary talks with the Belgian firm and agree an acceptable method of how the trade would go down. The selling price was disclosed to the Belgian firm who would seek agreement from the buyer. In that way the trade would go down between them and the Belgian guys.

The first meeting was in a motorway hotel. The Belgians had made their way there from the airport and booked a couple of rooms for the night. The UCO team had done the same but with no intention of staying the night as this was business, not a social meeting. They also knew there would be time for a few beers with their

European cousins later. The Plymouth team had no idea how many Belgians would arrive so they decided all four of them would travel to the motorway hotel. That was Neil, Dave, Robbie and Jimmy. Neil made a point of matching each one of them one for one at the meeting table, stipulating that any Belgian extra bodies would have to sit off to the side. That was designed to prevent the meeting being overcrowded and possibly to ruffle a few feathers.

Before the meeting, Neil said, "There's no reason to mistrust these guys, but Europeans tend to work a bit different to us and there is always a good chance they might bring guns to the meeting."

"That's most unlikely on this first meet as there is no valuable commodity at the venue," Dave interjected.

"Correct," Neil said, and set out a sort of batting order for the meeting. It was agreed that Dave and Neil would be one and two on the team with Jimmy in three and Robbie in four. Jimmy smiled at Robbie again. His face gave away his meaning as if he had said, "Me three, you four." Robbie, as imperturbable as ever, thought, *That's okay, Jimmy. I bet there are only two Belgian guys at the meeting so me and you will both sit it out.*

It was clear Jimmy was disappearing further down the rabbit hole as he was getting more involved, and the team were stroking his ego, not to mention stoking his sense of growing importance in the Plymouth firm.

As the four walked into the meeting venue, they saw two guys seated at a table close to the window overlooking the car park. They all guessed correctly. These were the men from

Brussels. One guy was mister average, nothing to write home about, but on the other hand, his mate was a contender for the stereotype of the 'muscles from Brussels.' He was huge, and as Jimmy later remarked, "A fucking big guy." Both appeared to be in their mid-forties and dressed like businessmen in smart trousers, jackets and open-neck shirts.

Neil and Dave followed the plan and sat *tête-à-tête* at a table with the two Belgians. Robbie and Jimmy sat at a separate table watching on. Once Robbie and Jimmy were seated at a separate table, and out of earshot of the four main players, Robbie whispered, "If things kick off, I'm fighting the little fucker, the hulk is yours."

Jimmy replied, "No worries, Robbie, the bigger they are the harder they fall. He won't know what's hit him." At that, they lapsed into a quiet fit of the giggles with them agreeing these two Belgians were now to be known as 'Tom' and 'Jerry', Tom being the bigger of the two. The Plymouth firm referred to them as that from then on.

The meeting went on for almost two hours over coffee and sandwiches with Robbie and Jimmy sat to one side. Jimmy insisted on keeping a close eye on Neil and Dave and positioned himself at his table with the best possible vantage point. Robbie thought, *Ten out of ten on the basic surveillance course, Jimmy. That's the position I would have taken up.*

As the meeting ended, all four at the main table stood up and shook hands with each other.

Tom and Jerry walked away in one direction. Neil and Dave walked towards Robbie and Jimmy. It was time for the long drive back to Plymouth with Jimmy at the wheel. On the journey back Neil went over the details of the meeting for the benefit of Robbie and Jimmy. Jimmy soaked it all in and occasionally asked a question or made a comment. Neil made a point of mentioning how professional the guys were and on the day of the race they would match them. He said he wanted them all suited and booted. This was a problem for Jimmy who didn't possess a suit.

On arriving back in Plymouth, Neil produced some folding from his pocket and handed some cash to Jimmy. "There you go, Jimmy, problem solved. Buy yourself a decent whistle but do me a favour and make sure it's black," Neil said.

The team purposefully allowed a few weeks to pass, during which time Jimmy would be engaged on his usual driving jobs, ferrying one or the other of Neil, Robbie or Dave around.

When driving Neil, he would feed Jimmy updates and bits and pieces on the development of the art job. Jimmy would tell the others in passing conversations. Neil had instructed Jimmy that on the day of the trade he was going to be with him and Robbie, together with Tom and Jerry and the art expert who was to validate the provenance of the painting. He told Jimmy he was to search all three for guns before they got into the hotel room with them and the painting. Jimmy's face was a picture. This role was icing on the cake. Later, Jimmy said to Dave, "Search them for guns? Now you're working in my sort of world."

Unlike the 'stolen' cigarettes, the painting was a fake. It was depicted as a genuine but stolen Lowry known as the *Factory Gates*. It had a cheap two-bob frame and even a casual scrutiny could have given the game away.

There were some misgivings within the UCOs and the cover team over this scam, so they decided to limit exposure to the 'stolen work of art', especially where Jimmy was concerned. In some ways, this exposure limitation was realistic because if it were the real thing, any professional gang would keep it under wraps as much as possible. Therefore, it was necessary for Neil to attend further notional meetings with Jimmy as the driver. Neil, in Jimmy's presence, had several cryptic phone calls about the trade to help reinforce the illusion. Those phone calls referred to a motorbike. Jimmy knew that was code for the painting, and he probably also knew this was common practice in the criminal fraternity to mask the nature of the real parcel. The deal was structured like this. Two hotels were picked on opposite sides of Exeter. One hotel for the Belgian money men and Dave plus another UCO called Dave who was drafted in for this play. A second hotel was for Neil, Robbie, Jimmy, Tom, Jerry, and their Belgium art expert plus the 'motorbike'.

The regular duo of Dave and Robbie stayed in a small bed and breakfast the day before the trade. The others were coming across with Jimmy the next day. Dave and Robbie enjoyed a couple of beers the night before and were up nice and early for the typical large English breakfast that put the 'breakfast' into the B&B abbreviation. Both had arranged to meet on the landing outside their rooms before going down for breakfast. They could not believe what they saw when they came onto the landing. Hanging there were three miniature prints. All three were Lowry's work and the middle one was the *Factory Gates*. On seeing them, Robbie said, "This bit of work is jinxed and has been since the Cover Officer walked in with the 'Lowry' weeks before."

By mid-afternoon on the day of the trade, all the Plymouth Operation George UCOs were in their respective locations. Jimmy and Neil were the last to arrive. Jimmy believed Dave was in his notional hotel awaiting the Belgian money men. He was, in fact, in a hotel room with the Cover Officer. Robbie and the other Dave were in the hotel room that was going to be used for the trade. Neil rang to inform them he was about five minutes away. That was a heads-up call to be ready with recording equipment on and running.

Following a light tap on the door, Jimmy and Neil entered Robbie and Dave's room. Jimmy walked in front of Neil who was smiling. Once Robbie took in Jimmy's appearance, he knew why there was a smirk on Neil's face. Jimmy's new set of clothes were black shirt, black trousers. black shoes and a three-quarter length black box jacket. It looked like one of those jackets you would see on the front of a 1960s pop album. Robbie said to Jimmy, "What the fuck is *that,* Jimmy? You look like one of the Beatles back in the sixties."

Jimmy was quick to defend himself and there followed some intermittent piss-taking between the four. Dave started to hum and sing every Beatle song he could recall. Jimmy carried on oblivious, justifying his choice and style. The next time Robbie saw this jacket was when he walked into the Crown Court in Belfast some six years later to give his evidence at Fulton's trial. Once the banter had died down, Neil placed a box in the wardrobe. He had carried the painting into the room wrapped in cloth and protected in an open box. A hush fell upon the room as Neil set about telling each of them what to expect and what he wanted them to do. He started by saying that Tom and Jerry, together with the expert, were to call Neil when they were in the reception. They had not been given the room number for security reasons. Once that call was made, Robbie and Jimmy were to go down to the reception and bring them up to the room using the lift. Once in the lift, Jimmy was to pat down all three for guns. Robbie was there to make up the numbers and if a gun was found he was to tell them that the deal was off and take the lift back down to the ground floor and then bid goodnight to their guests.

Neil's phone rang on cue and he had the conversation with Tom or Jerry. Robbie and Jimmy now made their way down from the third floor. On the way down in the lift, Jimmy looked at Robbie. He nodded and with a wink of the eye said, "Game on, Robbie, now you'll see how an operative works."

Robbie looked at Jimmy in his three-quarter length jacket and said, "Fuck off, Ringo." Both men burst out in laughter, struggling to regain their composure before the doors opened on the ground floor. Now straight-faced as the lift doors opened, they saw Tom and Jerry together with a third man who would act as their art expert. After the deed, and still in jocular mood, Robbie and Jimmy gave him the soubriquet of Lester – as in Lester the Tester.

Lester had a briefcase in his left hand and offered his other hand towards Jimmy, looking for a handshake. Jimmy declined the invitation and instructed the three to follow into the lift. The doors closed and Robbie pressed the button for the top floor. As he was doing so,

Jimmy directed the three men to stand to one side of the lift. He then asked the expert to open the case, which he did. There was nothing sinister in it. It contained some bottles containing clear liquids, brushes, a pallet knife, UV light, cloth, and some other small bits and pieces. Jimmy then patted him down face to face and once done got him to turn and face the wall of the lift and repeated the same routine down his back, sides, legs and arms. The same routine was carried out on Tom and Jerry. Jimmy looked like a dwarf next to Tom. The searching was complete by the time they reached the top floor. As the lift door opened, Lester made to step out. Jimmy gently tapped his arm and said, "No, no, my friend. We're not there yet." Robbie pressed the button for the third floor and off they went again.

The lift stopped on the third floor and Robbie led the way from the lift to room 302. A tap on the door and it was opened by Dave. Dave shared a greeting with Tom and Jerry and they in turn greeted Neil with a friendly handshake. Lester was introduced to Neil and explained he had some test kit with him. All this had been agreed at a previous meeting and phone calls between Tom and Neil. Lester asked if he may see the 'motorbike.' Neil took the box from the wardrobe and placed it on the bed and pulled back the cloth. Lester reacted as if he'd just clapped eyes on the Holy Grail. He asked Neil if he could take the painting into the bathroom to carry out a few tests to authenticate its provenance. Tom invited one of the English firm to accompany Lester, but Neil thanked him for the offer and declined as a show of trust and mutual respect.

About ten minutes later, Lester reappeared with the masterpiece wrapped in the cloth and placed it back in the open box. He turned to Tom and Jerry and gave his expert opinion that it was the genuine painting and worth every Euro. Tom called his man as Neil rang Dave in the other hotel. Tom spoke in Flemish to the mystery buyer. Jerry translated, telling them he was authorising the release of the money. Neil then told Dave to count the money and call back when happy. Twenty minutes later Dave rang to confirm that all the 'paperwork' was there, and all was good to make the exchange. Everyone beamed in that hotel room. There were handshakes all round, then the Belgians headed off into the sunset with their 'priceless Lowry.'

Jimmy beamed once more shortly afterwards as the Plymouth crime gang prepared to drive away. Neil called him over and handed him £500 in a bundle of banknotes saying, "Nice one, Jimmy. Not bad for very little work, eh."

# CHAPTER 19

## A Thousand Fags and Friction

Om Malik is quoted as saying[14], "As someone who has been wrong often, I can tell you one thing for sure: hindsight reminds you of your follies every day." So, at the risk of sounding foolish (not for the first time) perhaps hindsight tells us something about the subterfuge surrounding the 'stolen' work of art. It was risky. Clearly, there were no culture vultures as part of the operational team as it could be argued the choice of Lowry's *Factory Gates* was flawed in more ways than one. It had not been the subject of news reports telling all who cared that

---

[14] https://5quotes.info/quote/218656

it had been stolen, nor was it an enticing work, especially to involve overseas buyers. It was no fake Rembrandt or Holbein. It was also a cheap print in an even cheaper gilt frame. Hats off to these UCOs who pulled the wool over Jimmy's eyes, and who was obviously not much into culture himself. They got away with it. Sometimes one does... if the plan is audacious, and it was delightfully daring.

The Lowry plan, originally initiated by Mary, a Cover Officer, was a source of friction within the Plymouth UCOs. Naturally, Mary was keen on the plan and supplied the 'work of art', but others weren't convinced. As Mary produced the painting, some would have been thinking, *Okay, a painting. It's only a fucking Lowry, not any old Lowry but probably the most famous Lowry painting ever. She's turned up with the Factory Gates and it's in a ten pence frame that you'd pick up at a car boot sale. What is she thinking of? If this painting had been nicked it would be all over the six o'clock news and every newspaper in the fucking world.*

Neil piped up in a jovial tone, "Mary, are you pissed? A fucking Lowry! I know the square root of fuck all about paintings, but I know what that is before you tell me. It's like one of the most talked about paintings in modern time."

The team of UCOs all chipped in with a mixture of serious and piss taking comments and the tension coupled with the disbelief in Mary's choice of material lightened. Dave added, "Didn't they have a painting of a fucking horse eating grass in a field by John Stubbs?"

Robbie said, "George."

Dave again. "George? What do you mean 'George'? What the fuck are you on about, George?"

"George, his name is George Stubbs,' Robbie replied. "The guy that paints horses eating grass in fields, his name is George Stubbs, you fucking philistine."

The tension evaporated as the room burst into laughter, but it allowed Dave to think of a retort. "Fuck off, Robbie, you cock. You know who I meant, George fucking Stubbs. Una's dad, painter and decorator out of Watford."

The score was now two-one to Dave as all except Mary laughed at this side show. Mary frowned and tried to ignore the ribaldry. But Dave, sensing he was ahead, carried on. "What about a painting of a Cavalier wearing a big fuck off hat, drinking a pint at the bar?"

Cue more laughter, coupled with coughing, and choking noises from those sipping coffee or puffing on a cigarette. Everyone in the room could see that Mary wasn't joining in or enjoying being the butt of every joke. Neil brought the stand-up comedy show to a gentle end by saying, "We can work with this. We'll just be smart about what Jimmy sees and when he sees it. Thanks, Mary."

Dave thought, Yeah, thanks, Mary you've just made my job ten times harder. A fucking Lowry, for fuck's sake and Robbie, what's a fucking philistine?

This was a tight knit group of forceful characters who were all seasoned, nationally accredited undercover officers. They were living and working in a stress-filled atmosphere laden with potential danger to themselves, and possibly subconscious fears about the catastrophic consequences of operational failure. That last lengthy sentence and its precursor amounts to tinder awaiting the carelessly discarded match.

One of the UCOs knew trouble was brewing and the Lowry incident only served to reinforce his instincts. He didn't hit it off with Mary and often felt like he was skating on thin ice where she was concerned. As usual, the team got busy dreaming up a short 'bit of work.' That was their brief until such time they were told differently. The scam involved Neil who had a mate in Exeter who had asked him for a parcel of ten thousand fags as a favour and on the hurry up. Neil embellished the story by telling Robbie and Jimmy to jump in the car and make the delivery pronto as his mate was in a jam. Robbie was of course ready to react but Jimmy wasn't going to have much notice so he may have had to change his plans to accommodate Neil's request. The team saw that as a test of Jimmy's commitment to the firm and an effort to build up his role and status within it. The ops team and the Cover Officer directed that Robbie and Jimmy were to walk into a pub carrying two black bin liners stuffed with the fags. The plan then was for Robbie to recognise Neil's 'mate' and walk up to him. After a short conversation, the handover would happen. The parcel of fags in exchange for the agreed price, then Robbie and Jimmy were to exit the pub. That was the plan thought up and designed by the cover and ops team without any input from Robbie, the man on the ground.

Robbie in due course attended a briefing just before deployment. Mary, two members of the ops team and Robbie met in a hotel room. These officers represented the ops and cover teams plus the man on the ground. The plan was laid out and Robbie's role was explained as above. As the bit of theatre was being delivered to Robbie, it must have been clear to the others he was not happy as it was written all over his face. He looked at Mary and she seemed to have sensed Robbie's discomfort. At the end of the briefing the ops team asked if Robbie had any questions. He did.

"So, let me get this right. You want me and an Irishman to walk into a pub we don't know, and no one knows us. Carrying ten thousand fags in black bin bags. Sit at a table with another guy that no one knows in this pub. Conduct what can only look like a dodgy deal for cash in exchange for the fags. In front of everyone, including the landlord, and walk out. That's the plan?" Robbie's scathing contemptuous interpretation was the flame in the room full of petrol fumes. Nevertheless, he continued, "Okay, I'll do it. I think your plan is wonky, but if that's how you want it done, I'll do it just like that."

The proverbial pin dropped in the room. One of the ops team was first to respond and he invited Robbie to say what needed changing. Robbie took up the cudgel and stressed the optics of their plan of walking into a strange pub with a parcel of fags, and maybe the landlord's reaction to a criminal act on his premises. He added, "We're selling fags under his nose, and he might well be selling fags via a vending machine or from behind the bar at the real price. It's wonky." Instead, he suggested that Jimmy and he walk into the pub empty handed having left the fags in the boot of the car, meet with the buyer and have a drink together, making sure Jimmy was on soft drinks, then off to the car park and do the business out there; job done without disturbing the environment. All agreed. Robbie stood and walked out of the briefing and crossed the road to a café. His phone rang within a few minutes. It was Mary. She asked where he was and then asked him to wait there. A short time after Mary walked into the cafe and sat down. She said, "You have to stop arguing with the operational team, Robbie." He said, "Yeah, you're right, Mary. You should be doing it on my behalf."

The scam went ahead with no problems. Jimmy enjoyed being called on at short notice and given additional responsibility. During the journey he spoke about kneecapping people, again using the phrase, "Invite them round for tea." Robbie asked Jimmy to remind him never to come round his house for his tea.

## CHAPTER 20

## Torch the Trailer

Despite the friction, the scams continued. This time all concerned agreed on the latest bit of work. It was arranged that Robbie was going to do another lorry load. This time the parcel was going to be forty foot of booze. The deception was built around Robbie knowing a haulier who was struggling financially and needed a lump of cash on the hurry up. Robbie gave the non-existent haulier the name of Johnny who had a contract with a brewery company in Reading. The contract was pulling forty foot of booze from the brewery to the Tesco supermarket distribution warehouse in Southampton. Again, this was all designed so they could spend time with Jimmy, keeping him busy and under control and letting him disclose his evil deeds. At the same time, it reinforced the notion he was in with a proper firm of villains. It was a precondition of this scam that the lorry driver would have to be in the know on this, unsurprisingly, as they planned to heist not only the load but also steal the tractor unit and trailer. Furthermore, with Jimmy's presence they didn't want to use or threaten to use violence.

Neil set up a meeting with Robbie and Jimmy in the warehouse, the same one used for the cigarettes scam. Now acting out their respective roles, Robbie told Neil that he was going to have a further meeting or two with Johnny if needed and walk him through the way the job would go down. Robbie also told Neil that

Johnny was looking for £10,000 for his part in the theft. Neil said, "I'll start getting the booze placed with buyers. I know a good few who would be interested in cheap booze."

Robbie turned to Jimmy, saying, "I'll take you along with me on the day of the race to ride shotgun."

"Riding shotgun with you Robbie, I like the sound of that. Do I get a real shotgun?" Jimmy said.

Robbie smiling, looked at Jimmy and replied, "I wouldn't trust you with a super soaker sat next to me, you crazy fucking Irishman."

Neil, who was smoking a cigarette, burst into a fit of coughing and laughter. Now the scene was set, and Jimmy was walking into it with both eyes wide open.

Robbie reported back that he'd had his notional meetings with Johnny and his driver. He kept

Jimmy informed on the progress of the job, drip feeding him bit by bit. He told Jimmy that it would be a plain tractor and trailer. There were no markings or indication of what the load was. It was also a Scania tractor unit which made Robbie happy because he enjoyed driving that make and model.

Back at the office, the planning continued. A couple of scenarios were suggested by Neil, Robbie and Dave, another of the Plymouth UCOs. They included faking a Ministry of Transport routine check at one of the service stations. That was discarded. "Too many moving parts," commented Robbie. "Keep it simple, lads. He's giving it away, no need for a complicated high manpower plan. The driver has a time slot he must arrive at the warehouse. If, as on previous occasions, he is ahead of time he parks up short in a layby just off the M27 motorway. Jimmy and I have been up and had a look at the layby and it will be ideal. We will just take the keys off him. Jimmy and I will drive the load off to here and unload it. I'll need Hands for that and to drop me and Jimmy off around Southampton."

"Yeah, he knows a bit of work is in the offing," Neil replied.

"I've told the driver he'll be left tied up with a sack over his head nearby where he'll be found at least one hour after giving us a bit of a head start. I've told him exactly what to say to the old bill when they interview him. And it won't be the locals that deal with this, it will be those Regional Crime Squad boys," Robbie said. He continued, "I'll have a moody set of plates to stick on the tractor and trailer giving us that extra bit of comfort. We'll need a nicked motor to take the driver off in. Can I leave that with you, Dave?"

A nod of the head from Dave. "No worries, mate."

Robbie finished running out the plan. "Jimmy will have left his car here in the warehouse, so once we've tipped the load Jimmy can drive home. I'll take the empty trailer on a nice long drive up the motorway and ditch it. Dave can collect me and the job, as they say, is a good one."

Once all had been agreed, it was time to bring Jimmy into the further chit chats with each member of the firm, going over the finer details of their roles. Jimmy threw a suggestion in from left field. "Are you going just to ditch the lorry, Robbie? Why don't we burn the fucking thing?"

Robbie thought, Because, Jimmy my good man, that tractor and trailer belong to the Chief

Constable and he wouldn't be too pleased with Mr Colin Port if we were to do that.

Neil came to the rescue. "Nothing like having a fucking bonfire to let the old bill know where you are. You fucking idiot!"

The usual laughter and piss taking followed, with each giving and taking the banter. The meeting broke up with Jimmy driving Neil back to Plymouth. This bit of theatre was kept flexible as to timing, so keeping Jimmy on the hook. With Jimmy and Neil gone, Robbie got in the 24-valve Mondeo with Dave driving. Robbie knew this was likely to be another terror drive with Dave at the wheel of the Mondeo. Rumour had it that Dave and the Mondeo were on the local police traffic department's 'most wanted list.' Dave was an excellent driver and safe at speed. He had no time for lesser mortals so he would often inform and instruct other road users where they were lacking in his absolute best Anglo-Saxon English. "Fucking tosser, get out of the fucking way."

Eventually, the day for the bit of work was agreed. Jimmy drove Robbie to the warehouse where they met with Hands. A forklift truck and pallet truck had been picked up and were in the warehouse ready to go. Jimmy locked his car inside and all three set off for Southampton. Robbie carried two number plates which he tucked under the front passenger seat. The numbers were ghost plates which would match the tractor and trailer they were going to 'nick.' One set was fitted with thick rubber bungees that would go round and secure the plates over the original ones. That was intended to go on the back of the trailer. The front number plate was different as there was nowhere on the front of a tractor unit to affix the hooks at the end of a bungee cord. That plate had industrial strength double-sided tape running all the way along the perimeter of the inside of the plate.

The driver had been told to be in the layby at 8:00 pm, then switch off the engine and leave the keys in the ignition. He was also told to extinguish all the lights. The layby was just big enough to fit a lorry and trailer and at best two cars, eliminating the risk of another lorry's unwanted presence. Dave had got there early. Robbie, Hands and Jimmy arrived at around 7:45 pm. Parking their cars in the layby, they heard the lorry approach so both cars moved forward, allowing the wagon to pull up behind them. Jimmy and Robbie jumped out of the cars with Jimmy racing to the rear of the trailer to fit the new registration plate. Likewise, Robbie went to the front to fix the front plate. Johnny's haulage driver, following his instructions, got out of the cab passenger door and jumped into the back of Dave's car. By the time Jimmy had fitted the plate, the compliant driver was seen sitting in the back of Dave's car with a hessian bag pulled over his head. On seeing this, Jimmy jokingly said, "It reminds me of home." Robbie replied, "You're that ugly you'd need two sacks over your head." With that, Robbie climbed into the cab of the Scania to head for the warehouse where Hands would be waiting, ready to unload the twenty pallets at warp speed. Jimmy 'rode shotgun' at Robbie's side, filling the time on the journey with the telling of more stories of the life of an operator in Northern Ireland. It was all recorded on Robbie's hidden device.

On arrival at the warehouse Hands was ready to go. Robbie reversed the trailer into A1 position, without the assistance of Hands and his headlights this time. Jimmy was taking the cord out of the curtain side and pulling the curtain back. Hands was on the other side doing the same. Robbie went into the warehouse and came back out in seconds, driving the forklift. It was such a slick operation they didn't even have to talk to each other. They worked together like clockwork. Jimmy got in the warehouse and was guiding Robbie as to where the pallets should go. Jimmy used the hand-operated pallet truck to position the odd one that was slightly out of line, telling him that his boy could do a better job. The trailer was unloaded in record time. The warehouse was now locked and secure.

The trailer curtains were fastened, then Jimmy jumped into his car and shouted at Hands and Robbie as he drove away, "Happy days, boys."

Hands got into his car and followed Jimmy. As they approached a junction Jimmy indicated left and Hands right. Jimmy's car was being tracked in real time by the backroom staff, and once he was safely away they informed the Cover Officer, Gucci Gary, who in turn told the UCOs. Like all the other deployments, the Cover Officers dictated the play or called the shots as to exactly how the job was to be executed. The Cover Officers instructed the UCOs to reload the trailer ready to be later driven away by another driver (UCO). Robbie and Hands began the reload. After loading about fourteen of the pallets Hands did one of his famous shutdowns. Anyone who had worked with Hands will know exactly what that means. He just stares at you like one of those soldiers you see in those Vietnam war movies when they have been under fire for days on end – the thousand-yard stare. Hands was giving Robbie the stare.

He told Robbie, "Mate, I'm fucked, we'll finish this off in the morning." Hands was a supporting actor on this production and had there been Oscars for this operation he may have been a contender for best supporting actor. Robbie reminded him they were instructed to load the trailer and that is what they should do. Hands wasn't having any of it. With that thousand-yard stare he said, "I'll tell him [the Cover Officer], don't worry about it."

Robbie decided to play along with Hands as his colleague now looked like an anti-social psychopath from the film *One Flew Over the Cuckoo's Nest*. They locked down the trailer and made their way to Gucci's hotel room. It was getting late in the day. Gary was sitting in an armchair, smoking a posh fag, and had a pricey bottle of red on the go. Robbie had the impression Gary had been wearing a three-quarter length smoking jacket but had taken it off when he knew the UCOs were on their way. Gary asked how it went.

Robbie piped up, "Go on, tell him then. Mister fucking Sinatra."

Hands, still with that vacant stare, said, "I did it my way."

Gary said, "What do you mean you did it your way and why are you looking at me like that?"

Robbie chipped in, "We've got about another five or six pallets to load but he just zoned out on me and said he'd had enough for today. What can I do?"

Gary, a cheeky smile on his face, said, "You can get that fucking vacant look off your face and the pair of you get back down there and finish the job. I got a driver coming down in a few hours to pick it up and take everything back."

Hands had a quick coffee and after splashing cold water on his face he seemed to return to normal, or the nearest to normal in his case. Robbie could never work out what the issue was with Hands and the warehouse. Every time there was the combination of Hands and the warehouse something went wrong. He'd burnt out Robbie's retina with the car headlights. He zoned in and out of the job doing it like Sinatra in *My Way* and held up a ton of traffic driving the forklift, bringing unnecessary attention to himself.

CHAPTER 21

## On the Piss in Plymouth

There were occasions during the operation when Jimmy would stay over at the flat. It would usually follow a night out on the piss. The amount of alcohol consumed or tipped down Jimmy's neck was an area that his defence counsel would come to question and challenge during the trial. One of the team's major challenges was keeping Jimmy under control and keeping him occupied, to prevent him going rogue on the mainland. Imagine the consequences for Colin Port if Fulton committed a major crime, possibly a murder on the mainland whilst was being funded by 'UK Police PLC.'

That was not farfetched, just think back to his recent sojourn in the USA when he managed to get his hands on guns and explosives. Finding contacts on the British mainland to access guns and explosives would have been a walk in the park for this guy. So, keeping him busy was essential. In general, when a gang of criminals go out for the evening, they don't drink orange juice and talk about their holidays and families. There is no political correctness in their dialogue or lack of racist comments. They are people who live outside the law and acceptable societal standards.

The UCOs in the Plymouth 'firm' knew all conversations were recorded and many would be likely played in court at some future date. So, any one of them might laugh at a racist comment without endorsing it in the real world. It can be a difficult moment. When UCOs are on the plot, their thoughts are often working at warp speed. They are listening and responding in a natural way without facial expressions giving anything away and no unnatural delays in verbal responses.

Some experienced UCOs use the 'Two Ronnie's' technique to overcome these awkward moments. At the end of that TV show, little Ronny would sit in a chair to tell a story during which he would hop from topic to topic, telling a different story than expected. That's how some avoid answering a question or the need to comment on any given issue. As all humans are different, some naturally gravitate to this type of diversion and others initiate their own ruses to complement their character. Thinking quickly is the common denominator no matter the technique. It becomes second nature to a long-in the-tooth professional UCO. Another factor to be borne in mind, knowing all conversations are recorded, is the necessity to avoid direct questions. There must be no hint or semblance of any questioning or conversation that could be deemed as originating from an *agent provocateur*. This is not only for legal reasons, but a UCO does not wish to say something that makes the target think, *What the fuck did he just say?*

The plan with Jimmy was to manage his and the team's alcohol consumption. The UCOs would dump their drinks around the pub. For example, they would go over to the fruit machine and play a few bob and come back with no drink. On other occasions when Jimmy went to the loo, the drinks would be quietly disposed of. When Jimmy had finished his drink, they would move on to another pub leaving their unfinished drinks. The problem was Jimmy was not playing the game by following the same rules. Later at trial, the defence made a big thing about filling him up with alcohol in a futile effort to taint the admissibility of his admissions on the covert recordings. The team knew this was a soft underbelly for attack at any future trial by his defence team. Alcohol and evidence of admissions are bit like drinking and driving, not a good mix.

The listening post had picked up from the probe in Jimmy's Renault Laguna that he was possibly drink driving while not with any of the UCOs. Once again, this was a potential banana skin for Colin Port. Just imagine if he had killed someone whilst drink driving. The team were constantly reminded at briefings, and in particular Neil, to tell Jimmy not to drink and drive and attract attention to himself from the real police and thereby attract attention to the Plymouth firm. This missive came down from on high. Colin Port… balls of steel.

Notwithstanding the protocols and operating procedures, the team still had a job to do, and they were going to do it to the best of their abilities. So, it was natural for the team and Jimmy to go out on the piss; a gang of fellas enjoying spending their ill-gotten gains from their latest heist. They were celebrating. The beer, wine and good meals ordered and consumed was followed by more beer and a whiskey nightcap. Often at the end of the night take-away meals would be taken back to the flat. The UCOs would all be carrying recording devices that remained in place until one by one they made their excuses and left the company to retire to bed. On nights such as these, Jimmy would sleep on the sofa whilst the rest of them slept in a bedroom. Neil had the master bedroom because he was the boss. Robbie had a single bed in a small room. It was a flop, really. Just a place where the team got their heads down while in Plymouth. Sometimes, one of the UCOs would slink off and stay in a nearby hotel.

The Cover Officer at first insisted they hand over their recording devices and tapes before going to bed. The Cover Officer wanted them to leave the flat once they had pretended to go to bed and then hand over the stuff to prevent Jimmy having a sniff around and discovering the recording kit. No way was that going to work. With some low cunning and imagination, the UCOs found their own methods to do it their way.

One removed all his recording kit, including tapes, and placed it between the mattress and base of the bed. He figured that if Jimmy were to go looking for it, a fight would have broken out and he could bluff his way out without Jimmy finding the stuff. They also felt safe in the knowledge the flat was wired for live recording which meant someone in the listening post faraway would be monitoring Jimmy all night.

The morning after these nights out would typically involve Neil taking all the 'firm' including Jimmy to the Port O'Call café for the big boy's breakfast. Before leaving the flat, the UCOs secreted their recording devices and privately carried out the protocols ready to record the day's conversations with the target. Breakfast over, another day, another scam with Jimmy at the centre. That day's scam would have been scripted and agreed at a previous team meeting designed to give Jimmy the opportunity to talk over many hours. A case of 'here we go again.' Yet another trip down the rabbit hole and some scene changing in *The Truman Show*.

# CHAPTER 22

## Play Fighting

It became clear that Tanya and the kids were going to move to Plymouth after Jimmy found a home to rent. This big and new development brought its own challenges.

Once Jimmy had moved into his own Plymouth house together with his wife and the kids, extra problems arose. Play fighting with Jimmy Fulton's young son caused an issue on those occasions one of the UCOs visited Jimmy at his home. He was a lively little thing and always started to play fight, well they thought it was play fighting, but who knows? Robbie was the first to encounter the problem. He had a recording device strapped to him. Imagine it: the little tyke grabbing and pulling at him with his little arms around Robbie's legs, calling out, "Come on Robbie, let's fight." He felt like a postman trying to shake a yapping dog off his leg. It was worrying, so naturally it was up for discussion at a debrief, resulting in an SIO's policy decision that there would be no carrying of recording equipment when entering Jimmy's house. Ultimately, Colin Port would have signed it off as standard operating procedure (SOP). The UCOs on the team would also get to meet other members of Jimmy's family including his mother. The team perceived her to come from good stock. She carried herself well and dressed stylishly. She would often be seen sitting in an armchair, her back upright and not slouching. Sometimes, she would have the King James Bible on the armrest of her favourite chair. At least one of the UCOs found this hypocritical as he felt sure she knew what her sons were and what they had done under the banner of 'The Cause.'

Most of the team also met Tanya, Jimmy's wife. They figured Tanya and Jimmy had a volatile relationship, but she could hold her own with Jimmy. She benefited in many ways being married to him. Holidays were paid for from money which was either stolen, extorted, or donated to the LVF. There were kudos in being Mrs Fulton and the privileges that came with that title within their community. Tanya stayed in the UCO's Plymouth flat for a week's holiday before they found the house where Jimmy was later arrested. Tanya befriended a female who lived round the back of the flat during her holiday. This was important to the Plymouth team, knowing that she now had a new best friend living next door to them. They sharpened up on their tradecraft and behaviour while coming and going. They knew they had to be at the top of their game because it was impossible to know who might be connected to Jimmy and his wife via this new friend. Tanya was treated as an extension of her husband, and some viewed her an active member of the LVF after Jimmy told Robbie how he used her and their child in a pram to smuggle a firearm into the church at Drumcree. Jimmy also claimed the RUC wouldn't search her because of who she was. Whatever the truth of that claim, Tanya appears to have cashed in on her husband's name and reputation.

It was better all round for the Plymouth team after Jimmy, Tanya and their kids moved into the house on one of Plymouth's largest housing estates and mostly built in the post-WW2 era to accommodate many Janners, the regional nickname for Plymothians. Far removed from being a Janner, the relocation removed Tanya from proximity to the UCO's flat and gave the team, with the invaluable expertise of the technical team, opportunities to record conversations whether the UCOs were present or not. Just when things were looking up, the technical listening devices fitted in the house failed. The team was tasked with coming up with a ploy to get the family to vacate for a day while the tech people went into the place to fix it. More by accident rather than design Robbie had already got the solution: fitting coving to the ceiling.

The previous occupant of Jimmy and Tanya's house had coving fitted to the lounge ceiling and walls. Sometime later, an occupant had removed the coving and it looked a mess with the painted walls stopping short of the ceiling. Robbie had mentioned to Jimmy a few times that Jimmy should replace the coving or redecorate the room. Tanya also got on Jimmy's case about it. Robbie didn't waste time in telling the Plymouth team that he was a dab hand at DIY. In a former life, he had gained qualifications for painting and decorating. Who would have thought when he completed his City and Guilds it would become a tool in the toolbox of his undercover career?

The fledgling plan was developed. Fledgling… and cunning, like Baldrick – he of "I have a cunning plan" in the *Blackadder* comedy show. Jimmy was to drive Neil to Exeter for a business meeting. As a treat, Neil invited Tanya along for lunch, promising he would pay. Possibly the real cunning part, Jimmy was to be brought in on the plan under the guise of surprising Tanya when they got back from Exeter and finding the coving done. He was told to leave a key under the door mat so Robbie could let himself in. What neither Jimmy nor Tanya knew was Robbie would bring the tech team along with him. Once the job was done, Robbie was to replace the key under the mat and leave the house: coved, clean, tidy and fully wired for clear audio product.

At one stage Dave was going to do the coving with Robbie, and Robbie was happy about that. However, Dave – with his great command of the English language, used his stock phrase, "Fuck off," before adding, "I'm an undercover police officer, not a lackey to some Irish terrorist. I'm not doing it."

A hush filled the room. You could cut the atmosphere with a blunt knife. Robbie piped up and broke the deadly silence with, "No worries, I can do it alone." Everyone in the room began to breathe again.

As for Dave, it was water off a duck's back. He was quite within his rights to turn down the proposal. The meeting broke up and the plan was actioned for the following day. In preparation, Robbie headed off to B&Q for the tools, fixings and lengths of plaster coving. Neil called Jimmy and arranged the trip to Exeter with Tanya after they had dropped their lad off at school. The technical boys were put on standby. Dave arranged to take the day off.

The following day the plan sprang into action. Jimmy, accompanied by his wife, set off in the car from his house to pick up Neil from the city-centre flat. At the same time Robbie set off for Jimmy's house. It is feasible Jimmy and Robbie must have passed each other at some point. Robbie arrived at Jimmy's and found the key as arranged. Letting himself in, he left the door on the latch as he went to and from his car to collect the tools and materials. The technical team also entered to do their stuff at this time.

Robbie cracked on with fixing the coving. He tackled the most difficult first: the awkward cuts and angles like around the chimney breast and around a few pipes running from the ceiling to the floor and onto the radiators. He left the easier long straight runs of coving until the end. He knew they could be done with speed and fewer cuts. They had an idea of the time Jimmy and Tanya were to return home and the technical team had finished with about an hour to spare. Not that they were too worried as Neil had them both under control and they were confident that Neil would have warned Robbie if there were any unforeseen hiccups.

That was viewed as luxury by the tech team as it wasn't often they were afforded that type of protection. Showing their gratitude, they gave Robbie a hand finishing the long straight runs of coving and cleaning up. Both of those tasks are best carried out by more than one pair of hands. It was excellent teamwork. No one disturbed the environment or attracted attention to themselves.

Later that day and after Jimmy and Tanya had returned home, Robbie received a phone call from Tanya in which she thanked him for the surprise. She was also complimentary about the standard of workmanship and pleased there was no mess.

Robbie made light of it by saying, "No problem. I was in the area, my pleasure." Neil, Robbie and Dave went out for a beer that night and perhaps unsurprisingly considering Dave's earlier outburst, the day's activities were never mentioned. The revamped audio was working again. Now, to catch Jimmy in the act.

# CHAPTER 23

## Swinger

Mark 'Swinger' Fulton was the leader of the Loyalist Volunteer Force (LVF), having taken over its command following the assassination of Billy Wright in the Maze Prison in 1997 by members of the Irish National Liberation Army (INLA).

Journalist Susan McKay alleged Fulton carried out a dozen sectarian killings in the 1990s.[15] During the operation, Jimmy's family from Northern Ireland would come and visit him. As well as Tanya's visits, Jimmy's mother would make trips over. She was a well-presented

---

[15] https://belfastchildis.com/tag/mark-fulton/

woman. She came from good stock and her style and manner of speaking underlined this. Her manner of dressing, her deportment and her command of the English language all bore testament to her good upbringing.

But the visitor from Northern Ireland who was a real person of interest was Jimmy's brother, Mark Fulton, known by many as Swinger. He had recently been released from jail after serving a term for a terrorist offence along with Billy Wright. Jimmy had invited Swinger to see him in Plymouth saying, "Come and meet my new mates, the Plymouth firm. They are good boys and bang at it. What's more, they pay well." Swinger accepted, but this caused a kerfuffle in Colin Port's MIT back in Belfast, not to mention in London. Not only did they now have one paramilitary terrorist on the mainland, but the prospect of two of the deadliest running around the mainland hand in hand, maybe itching to pick up from where they had left off. Worse, if things did start to go *boom* on the mainland, many would have rightly observed it was all sponsored by 'UK Police PLC.'

After returning to Belfast and following the arrest of his brother, Jimmy Fulton, he committed suicide while in custody awaiting trial. He was found dead in his prison cell at Maghaberry Prison and possibly could not face the rest of his adult life in prison. Either that, or he was embarrassed the leader of the LVF had been duped by a handful of undercover cops. It's strange being ensnared by undercover officers is not something prisoners brag about on the streets of Northern Ireland nor on a wing inside a high security prison.

By the time of Swinger's visit, Jimmy was living in the house in Plymouth. Before he moved in the technical team had wired it from top to bottom with listening and recording devices. The two brothers also visited Muriel in Cornwall where the electronic eavesdropping continued. Neil, as boss of the firm, made it clear to Jimmy he must take some time off whilst his brother was visiting. He said, "Jimmy, son, when your brother comes across, I want you to enjoy yourself. Take some time off and catch up on things. We'll be okay for a few days or a week or so without you. I got some family stuff to take care of so no worries."

Jimmy was grateful for this act of friendly kindness and was quick to say so. "That's good of you, boss. But you'll have to meet up with him while he's here. He's a good man and good operator [the word he used to describe a paramilitary member] and you never know, he might be looking for a job now that's he's out and on the straight and narrow."

Robbie chipped in. "Yeah, that's a fucking good idea. Jimmy, my man, you can take us out for a Chinese and you can pay."

Jimmy said, "For fuck's sake, Robbie, I paid for the tea in the caff this morning. It's fucking your turn to pay."

This banter produced much laughter and a degree of piss taking. But Neil and Robbie had that feeling of internal satisfaction and professional pride that they had just laid out the blueprint to the next chapter in *The Truman Show* starring Swinger Fulton. *Poor Jimmy, you just don't get it*, they thought. *We want you and Swinger together enjoying yourself, relaxing and talking over old times.... that's not kindness, Jimmy, it's just good old bill.* Human nature is human nature. We all do similar things and have similar character traits when it comes to meeting up with family and friends we haven't seen for some time. We bring them up to date on what we've been up to and talk about old times, and that was exactly what they did.

Owing to the sterile corridors of covert policing, the team imagined Swinger left Belfast in the company of a surveillance team and was picked up on the mainland by the same Belfast-based team but with different faces. Most working undercover cops love surveillance. Many get a kick out of following someone for days on end, gathering evidence.

Operation George was different. They were not following anyone. They had invited Jimmy into a parallel world that they controlled and sealed it off as if it were a vacuum. He was like a goldfish in a bowl they had made.

Jimmy collected Swinger from Bristol airport in the all singing, all dancing wired-for-sound Laguna. The flight was direct from Belfast to Bristol with EasyJet. This visit also gave the team a little respite as they had little to do with them over the period he was there. But the main operational team did not sleep. There was around the clock monitoring by fixed probes and mobile probes together with Swinger's Belfast watchers. Yet, there was one memorable evening, prompted by the earlier banter about the Chinese meal.

There was a Chinese restaurant in the square close to the flat used by the UCOs. Like all good UCOs, the Plymouth team built a rapport with the management and staff by being frequent big spending customers. This was designed to give the impression to other diners that they were local, and this was their 'go to' restaurant. Over time, they built the restaurant into their deep cover so that by the time Swinger walked in there with them it was clear the team were 'real people' who belonged and were popular and respected within the local community. They didn't portray themselves as loud and cocky, the sort of guys that would annoy and or disturb other diners. They were friendly, polite and likeable guys. They didn't disturb the environment.

Swinger bought straight into this illusion. He applied the trick to himself. The friendly restaurant owner had arranged a table in a corner, off to one side; it was perfect. The position of the table meant that all could talk freely and openly about their 'business' and the Fultons could do the same without others hearing a thing. Swinger came down the rabbit hole.

The UCOs took a listening device into the restaurant and in addition the UCOs were recording all conversations with separate hidden recording equipment. The listening device was for officer safety. It allowed a monitoring team to listen in to the conversation and react if it all went tits up at the table and Swinger were to go into one and kick off violently. They knew Swinger was more volatile than Jimmy, so the cover and the operation teams insisted on this listening device being deployed.

They all met up in a local pub close to the restaurant and introduced themselves to Swinger. He looked like the typical LVF member. Pictures of Billy Wright, James Fulton and Swinger Fulton made them look like brothers. They all had the same hair style, same build, same style of dress, same tattoos and the same strong Northern Irish accent. They were like clones of each other. Swinger came across as a bit of a thinker.

Both Fultons extolled Billy Wright's virtues and what a great orator he was and how the British government had him killed (the murder was attributed to the Irish National Liberation Army – INLA) because he was unafraid of the government or anyone else in that case. Swinger was in jail at the time of Billy Wright's murder and Jimmy had to arrange the illegal and unauthorised paramilitary funeral – a bunch of men and youths would congregate, dressed in a mish mash of military type uniforms, wearing balaclavas and sunglasses to hide their identities and marching like youngsters in the Boys Brigade. At the graveside a mixture of firearms would be produced, rifles and pistols, then a volley of shots fired over the coffin of the poor unfortunate lately departed terrorist. Amen. The team sat straight faced as Jimmy spoke about how he organised this 'military operation' and mentioned the names of the pall bearers. One was Philly who lived near Bristol at this time. The team later tried to pull Philly down the rabbit hole, but he never accepted the invitation which came straight from Jimmy's lips. On one visit to Jimmy's house, he produced a photograph of the cortege in the sunglasses and balaclavas, standing by the coffin. He very kindly pointed at each of them and named them for the record.

Back at the restaurant, the UCOs sat at their 'special table.' There was Neil, Dave, Robbie, Jimmy and the new cast member, Swinger. The listening device was placed naturally and deftly in the middle of the table, together with phones and sundry bits and pieces, including the usual crockery and cutlery. The sundries also included things like spectacles cases, fag packets, lighters, car keys cluttering the table. Free space was now at a premium.

Swinger, without notice or warning, decided the table needed sorting out. He picked up the item containing the listening device to move it. The three UCOs breathed a collective deep breath and thought in unison, *Fuck! What's he picked that up for?* Robbie said later, "I thought, has it got a little red light flashing showing it's on a call? Bollocks, stand by for action. It's all going to go off at Haydock any second now."

No doubt all three wondered what the listeners were thinking as they tried to interpret what the change in sound was all about. Their thoughts were rushing at something approaching Mach One speed. Within seconds panic subsided.

Swinger had placed the device on a small shelf next to his head. The UCOs couldn't have re-located it to a better position. *There is a god*, Robbie thought as he downed a large mouthful of fine wine. In addition to them talking about Billy Wright and the LVF, the UCOs gently steered the conversation to finding some work for Swinger within their gang. He didn't dismiss the proposition but wanted to consider his options after he returned to Northern Ireland. They didn't push the subject any more than that. A great night was had by all, the meal finished, and they all went their separate ways.

The team wasn't to see Swinger again. He finished his visit and returned home to Portadown where he remained until his arrest in June 2001. He was found dead in his prison cell at HMP Maghaberry, Northern Ireland on 10 June 2002.

# CHAPTER 24

## Barbara Windsor

Neil and Jimmy set off on the long journey back to Plymouth from one of their trips to London. Starting out on the A4, which is always slow with heavy traffic, they then headed on to the M4 towards Bristol. Neil had worked out that his tape would need changing around Chieveley Services, situated on the M4 close to the A34 junction. He figured this could take between an hour and a half to two hours depending on traffic. Once they clear the A4 and hit the M4 motorway, Jimmy hit a cruising speed of between seventy and seventy-five miles per hour. Neil always insisted on this maximum speed to avoid traffic stops and attention from the 'real police.' Jimmy knew which side his bread was buttered so complied. On one of the first such journeys along this route, Neil had pointed out to Jimmy two mobile masts in the middle of woodland adjacent to the motorway on the eastbound Carriageway near Chieveley Services. These masts were disguised to look like trees so that they didn't stick out and spoil the natural environment. Jimmy must have been impressed, for he never tired of repeating the story and pointing at the disguised masts to whomsoever happened to be in the car with him. He was fond of saying, "How clever is that? Imagine disguising them as trees." *Masts? Trees? Undercover officers?* Another piece of irony. Back to their journey, where Neil was aware that his two hours were almost up. He asked Jimmy to pull in at the next Services so he could have a coffee and a leak. Jimmy, as always, agreed.

On arriving at Chieveley and after Jimmy made refence to the disguised masts for what felt like the millionth time, Jimmy parked up in the furthest space away from the entrance. Neil gave Jimmy a sideways look and asked Jimmy to call a taxi for him.

"A taxi? What do you want a taxi for, boss?" Jimmy asked.

"To get me to the fucking door. Go and park up by the building, you wanker," came the reply. Jimmy knew that was just Neil's sense of humour, so no offence was taken. He drove over to the disabled parking bays right by the entrance to the building. As both men alighted and were walking to the Services entrance doors, Neil spotted Barbara Windsor coming down the steps towards the car park. He nudged Jimmy and pointed in her direction.

"Look who that is coming this way."

Jimmy said, "Where? Who?"

"The two women walking towards us; the one in the purple leather jacket and trousers. It's Barbara Windsor."

"Oh! fuck me, so it is. I'm going to ask her for an autograph."

On approaching the two women, Jimmy shouted out in that heavy and distinct Northern Irish accent, "Hey! Babs, what about a wee autograph?"

This request was so loud it attracted the attention of other members of the public in the area and everyone turned to look towards Jimmy and Neil.

Don't attract attention, thought Neil, Fucking good job, Jimmy. We've got the whole population of Berkshire looking at us.

The lady accompanying the celebrity, possibly Ms Windsor's agent or a management team member, looked directly at Jimmy. Shock and surprise were etched over her face. She took Barbara's elbow and guided her away with an understandable excuse that they were running late and had to dash. Unabashed, Jimmy added a few more requests for an autograph while the agent steered Barbara away from this loud insistent Irishman.

Both men entered the Services building. Neil handed Jimmy a tenner and asked him to get the coffees. Taking the cash, Jimmy made his way to the self-service counter as Neil headed off to the toilet to do what the stop was really all about. Leaving the toilets, Neil could see Jimmy just paying for the drinks. Neil, now holding his mobile phone to his ear spoke in hushed tones. "Today's date is Friday the 12th of May 2000 and the time is 4:20 pm. I'm at Chieveley Services on the M4 motorway and I am just going to re-join Jim at the table." Both men arrived at a table at the same time as Neil finished his phone conversation with, "Yeah, we've just pulled in for leak and a coffee. We should be back down there in a few hours, Robbie. I'll call you then, mate. Okay?"

Phone off. Tape changed, coffees on the table. It's showtime again. *Quiet please, places everyone, lights, camera and action.*

Coffee done, and back into the car, they continued their journey to Plymouth. The M4 turned into the M5. The Highways Agency were carrying out major repair works on the motorway bridge that spans the River Avon. It was guaranteed to slow down the journey time, but once across the bridge it almost feels like you are nearly home. They stayed on the M5 until it finished at Exeter where it runs into the A38 down to Plymouth, taking them by the Little Chef where Dave and Robbie shook off surveillance. Neil was aware another tape change was needed before Plymouth. The area surrounding Cullompton in Devon was a favoured location by all the UCOs for such changes. It is about two hours driving from Chieveley, traffic permitting. There were a few suitable places around there so the UCOs would chop and change the locations, so Jimmy didn't start forming a pattern in his head. At debriefs, the UCOs would always mention where they had stopped and changed tapes, so everyone knew to mix it up. Good tradecraft. On arrival in Plymouth, Neil would follow his usual routine of paying Jimmy for his day's work, then Jimmy would drive home under control of the tracker and listening device fitted to his car. That was the end of a typical day's deployment but not the end of the working day for the UCOs. The paperwork needed doing. Notes to be made. Tapes to be marked up with exhibit identification marks and either a hot debrief to the Cover Officer or a full debrief with the operational team depending on the time, location, and operational necessity.

As an aside, notes in an undercover officers' pocket notebooks in a situation like Operation George are intended as an *aide memoire.* They are not for filling with copious notes, and it isn't a good practice. The contemporaneous record of the deployment is the tape.

Once all the 'admin' had been taken care of it was time to relax and unwind after a day of listening to Jimmy talk about his activities and horrendous crimes whilst in Northern Ireland. It had been another day of thinking, *How do I get him to disclose more without asking him a direct question? How do I get him back on to that subject?* In Jimmy's company it felt like the brain was processing information at high speed, listening, reacting, thinking of tradecraft, and countless other thoughts: *How much recording time have I got left? What's the rules of evidence around my questions? Can I say this?* The list was endless, and each deployment with Jimmy had to be managed on its own merits.

# CHAPTER 25

## Paranoia

Working undercover for any length of time can make the most stable people become paranoid. Over time and since the Operation Julie days of the Seventies, the police service has recognised the need for psychological support for UCOs owing to the often dangerous, difficult and stressful roles they undertake. They must attend appointments with a psychologist at regular intervals. Indeed, the Operation George UCOs were offered professional help on tap if they felt they required support. In modern times, a new UCO would pay a first visit to see the professional, usually a psychologist, soon after s/he has completed and passed the National Undercover Course.

In the words of one undercover officer, "I attended an office block in London and checked in with the receptionist using a moody name and informed her I had an appointment with Mr Smith (not his real name). After a few minutes, a small wiry guy came down and spoke to me using the moody name then led me to his office. Mr Smith sat down with a pen in his hand with a writing pad on a coffee table in front of him. Unsure how to kick off the session, I said, 'What do you want to know?'

"He said, 'Anything you want.'

"'Well, what do you know about me?'

"'I know your National Number and that's all. I don't even know your name, just a number.'"

That was the start of a long relationship between that UCO and the psychologist. By the end, the psychologist knew more about that UCO than any other person on the planet. He kept a file full of notes completed with fresh material after each visit. The officer shared information about his family, his jobs, police life, and private life except for his extra marital affairs. "Some things are too private to share," he added. Such appointments were scheduled every six months. Everything shared is strictly confidential, not even shared with police management unless it was thought you were unstable, or a threat to yourself or others; then he was duty bound to tell your line manager. Back to the anonymous undercover officer who told this story. "The only time I showed any emotion with him was when I recounted an incident that took place whilst I was on holiday. I saw a child aged about five or six lying on the bottom of the swimming pool. It turned out the pool attendant, who wasn't a lifeguard, went to rat's shit and did fuck all other than panic. He was screaming and running around like a headless chicken. My training kicked in and with another Brit I got the lifeless body out of the pool and started working on him. You know, mouth to mouth and CPR on this kid. He started to breathe then vomit all over the place. I turned the kid into the recovery position and forced his mouth open to clear his airway. I'd never done that before on a real person and I was surprised how difficult it was to open the casualty's mouth.

"A crowd of Spanish and Brit onlookers surrounded us and started giving me shit for forcing his mouth open and sticking my fingers into his mouth to clear his airway. The ambulance came and took over. The kid was in hospital overnight and after that he was back on site and in the pool. It was some time after I got a bit of PTSD. I kept thinking what would have happened if my efforts to revive him had failed. I was recounting this story to the shrink through floods of tears. It was the only occasion I showed or even felt any emotion in front of him."

## Police National Computer (PNC)

As far back in the early days of undercover policing, UCOs sometimes got paranoid. It may be the case that it comes with the territory because of deception and duplicity becoming the norms. Take Bentley in his pioneering Operation Julie days, for example. For a long time, he harboured a serious belief that the two characters he met on the cocaine importation plot in Liverpool were themselves undercover agents for a rival law enforcement agency, either in the UK or the States.

On Operation George, Robbie and Jim Fulton were the only ones who knew of the registration number of the tractor unit. But it was checked by way of the RUC and the Garda as part of a batch of ten vehicle registration numbers. This lorry on that number had only been out once before, and that was a week before when Robbie and Jim took it out for a dry run of the job they were planning. Before Robbie had driven it or Jim had ridden in the cab, a guy delivered it and told Robbie the number had been PNC checked. The guy knew nothing and had no idea of what Robbie was engaged in. All he was doing was delivering a lorry to him at a service station on the M25. Robbie, thinking it was strange, started to drive to Weston-Super-Mare, planning to park the tractor unit on an overnight lorry park. Thinking more about the brief conversation about the PNC check,

Robbie called the ops team. He told them the story and they assured him they would investigate it.

Still bothered, Robbie then called Dave. "Mate, come to Gordano Services on the M5. Don't approach me though, we'll chat on the phone once you get there but make sure you eyeball me because I need you as a third eye." On arriving at the services area, Robbie called again. Dave now had Robbie and the tractor unit in sight. Between them they hatched a counter-surveillance plan for Robbie to drive out, followed by Dave as the third eye.

After a while and still in contact over the phone, Dave said, "There's nothing. Can't see anything. Nothing at all."

It is difficult to conduct counter or anti-surveillance in a tractor unit or a lorry with trailer behind because the lorry isn't fast enough to get away. So Robbie instructed Dave to get off the motorway and make his way to a choke point to see if anyone was following the lorry. Once more, Dave reported he had seen nothing. Robbie now drove into the lorry park in Western-Super-Mare, but not before he had driven through a normal car park designed for only cars. At the far side of the regular car park is where all the heavy lorries and coaches park up overnight. Dave still followed. Robbie looked everywhere, as he was still in anti-surveillance mode. He looked right, left, straight ahead, checked his mirrors and looked overhead. Then, he saw an overpass: a service road straddling the car park. More importantly, he then saw a man and woman sitting in what appeared to be a four-door, two-litre car. She had a handbag over her shoulder and it seemed to Robbie she was looking for something inside the bag. *Typical female surveillance ruse*, thought Robbie, *she's got a covert radio stashed in the bag*.

Robbie glanced up again at the flyover and spotted a bloke eating from what looked like a bag of fish and chips. With that, he spoke to Dave over the mobile phone. "Looks like we have just driven into a choke point."

Dave said, "Yeah, I see him and the car."

Robbie said, "Let me park up then I'll get my overnight bag. Then I'm going to walk up to your car." Robbie did that and on getting into Dave's car, he said with a smile, "Come on, we'll have a bit of a laugh on this." Robbie opened his bag. Dave, acting out the role, peered into it, poked inside and started grinning, giving lots of thumbs up signals as if it were a parcel, before placing the bag in the boot. The bait in place, Dave drove off in the 24-valve Ford Mondeo.

The fish was hooked. The Mondeo was followed out of the car park.

What the followers did not know was that Dave was one of the most wanted drivers in his force area. Wanted because he was fast but safe. Robbie, if asked, would have put it a different way: "He drives like a nutcase!"

Dave gunned that car all the way from Weston-Super-Mare south-west down the M5 until he reached the Little Chef next to Exeter Racecourse, covering the sixty miles or so in much less than an hour. There was still a Golf GTI on his trail, so Dave pulled into the car park of the Little Chef. The GTI driver was now on his own and utterly compromised, so he turned around and left the car park. He didn't go in the restaurant nor the petrol station next door. He simply disappeared. It was time for a debrief.

At the debrief, the operational team downplayed the possibility of a team on them. In fact, they dismissed the idea completely out of hand. For weeks after the car chase, Robbie kept asking for any updates on the surveillance. No, was the stock answer and Robbie was urged to 'move on.' It seemed they just wanted it to treat it as a 'sleeping dog.' But when one adds up all the unusual spooky events, Robbie felt it was more than a possibility. He knew what surveillance looked like, so he was convinced some other team or outfit was watching him and the Operation George team. As soon as he drove into that lorry park, he saw them.

The morning after the race to Exeter, Dave and Robbie drove to the flat in Plymouth. As they came off the main dual carriageway they got picked up by a surveillance team again. In haste, they made towards the flat. Robbie and

Dave clocked the same car that had taken up position behind them coming off the dual carriageway. Dave made a quick left into a square and they watched the car drive on by. They both suspected some foot men may have lain in wait near the flat, so they carried on driving out of the square to head for the Port O'Call café. Dave parked up outside before they went in and ordered two big boy breakfasts. The UCOs were not at all surprised to see a stranger enter the café on his own. He took a seat and was joined by a female some three or four minutes later. They too ordered the big boy breakfasts. Robbie and Dave waited for them to be served with their breakfasts. As soon as they were placed on the table, Dave and Robbie got up and walked out the café. They had burned them. All activities were cancelled that day because Dave and Robbie maintained they were under surveillance, despite the ops team denying it.

Besides Robbie, the only person who had prior knowledge of that lorry registration number was Jimmy. That provoked some theories: one, Jimmy might've served it up for some reason no one could explain. Two, some other law enforcement organisation had taken interest in the paramilitary terrorist. Three, perhaps MI5 had set a team of watchers on to them. Robbie felt somehow these clandestine activities had contaminated him via the lorry. He wondered if that was how the lorry registration got fed into the PNC. Or maybe it was just a coincidence or a typo along the line somewhere. But, deep down, he knew something was wrong.

The team cancelled what it planned that weekend and they decided to move the job to a later date. When the plan was reactivated, a fixed-wing aircraft followed the lorry at a discreet distance. During the journey with Jimmy in the cab of the lorry, Jimmy got talking to Robbie about police surveillance back in Northern Ireland. At one point, he said, "Don't you worry, Robbie, I can smell the police." Little did Jimmy know he was sitting next to one and with another one flying above his head. Some on the Operation George team reflected on this strange episode years later. One was convinced there was bound to have been twenty-four-hour surveillance on Swinger, Jimmy's brother, if not in the form of the many listening devices deployed, as a surveillance team to cover him moving under his own steam from A to B. Some were also convinced looking back that some parts of the jigsaw didn't quite fit. And possible explanations for things that seemed like minor miracles at the time. It was

Robbie's guess this surveillance team may have been used on other aspects and events on the job. For example, the ghost team that Robbie and Dave experienced in the chase to Exeter and the café the next day, the god sent car that made space outside Jimmy's house the night before his arrest. And, later, you will read about the big fella Robbie met in a Belfast hotel. If you work undercover for a long time, you get those intuitions. You know when something doesn't smell right. As they say, if it looks like a duck and quacks like a duck, it's a fucking duck.

### Jimmy and the RUC Officer

Throughout the UCOs' operational deployments and the hundreds of hours of recordings captured from house and car probes, Jimmy never admitted to the murder of Rosemary Nelson. It was a common feature at most debriefs for the UCOs to report Fulton claimed that she was killed by the British Government. He never once indicated or claimed that he did it or ordered the murder. He repeatedly pointed towards the British Government in collusion with the military, police and security services. Jimmy didn't hesitate to talk about all the offences he was eventually indicted for.  Most of the team believed if he were culpable in any way for Rosemary Nelson's murder, he would have disclosed it to the team in one of the many captured conversations. In Fulton's bloated self-esteem, it would have been a massive feather in his cap and great kudos. So the Plymouth Operation George team believed Jimmy didn't do it nor have any knowledge of who did. Coupled with the collusion statements about the British authorities being instrumental in Nelson's murder, Jimmy also spoke often about an RUC officer. He did name him, but the authors choose not to reveal his name or rank. Jimmy always spoke in high regard of this officer and talked about meeting him in Northern Ireland on several occasions. The meetings didn't take place in police stations, but they were the sort of venues and environments that a seasoned informant handler would choose for a meeting. The team gained the impression that their relationship was that of informant and handler. This situation on the mainland would have warranted someone like Jimmy to be registered as a 'Dangerous Informant.' He would be seen as high-risk by any informant handling controller owing to him being a known terrorist. It is likely the rules about handling informants in Northern Ireland may have been different. On the mainland, it would not have been good practice or policy to meet someone of Jimmy's character alone. Meetings with 'Dangerous Informants' are always two handed. Accurate contact reports would be completed immediately after the contact and both officers would sign the report and it would be submitted to the controller. Despite those policy and practice differences, in the opinion of some of the team, this RUC officer's relationship with Jimmy was totally professional and many believed that Jimmy was possibly a snout – an informant. One of the disclosures Jimmy made to the UCOs about the RUC officer was that he (Jimmy) handed over four ounces of explosives to the officer at a clandestine meeting. Jimmy told them it was the same amount of explosives that was used to killed Rosemary Nelson. Jimmy went on to claim that the explosives were taken from a secure police storage facility and used in the bomb. All of this was dismissed as a figment of Jimmy's imagination and another attempt to bolster the conspiracy theories surrounding the death of Rosemary Nelson. It was, however, recorded in the debriefing notes.

Of course, any mention of Rosemary Nelson by our target would reach the eyes and ears of Colin Port. He was in the habit of visiting the Plymouth officers about once a month to inform the group how things were progressing. The team valued these visits which were another component of Colin Port's excellent leadership skills. He didn't have to attend; he could have sent one of his Senior Management Team (SMT). But he took the trouble to sit down with the detectives who were walking a dangerous line day in and day out. At the end of each meeting Colin Port would ask if anyone had any questions. There were the normal serious questions and a few funnies. The meetings were always relaxed and if a stranger had walked in, God forbid, they wouldn't know Colin Port was a Deputy Chief Constable (DCC). During one of the question-and-answer sessions, Colin Port was asked by one of the UCOs about the RUC officer. The UCO asked if much was known about the officer and what, if any, was the relationship between him and Jimmy. Without any hesitation, Colin Port replied with words to the effect of: "If I had any concerns about the officer, he would not be involved in this enquiry. He has my full confidence."

His reply was like an explosion in the room. Heads dropped amongst the Cover Officers and operational team. They avoided any eye contact with the UCOs. For their part, the UCOs all looked at each other open mouthed. Colin Port continued with words of confidence in the character of the officer.

Then one of the UCOs asked if the RUC officer knew about them and their role with Jimmy. Port told the assembled team that he knew they were undercover officers. He knew their pseudonyms but had no idea of their real names or where they were from.

This development was surprising and unusual, but the collective wisdom and reasoning of all in the room was if Colin Port was good with the situation so were they. They knew Colin Port as an outstanding leader, and he had the full confidence of every team member no matter their role. It was obvious that they (the Belfast MIT) had been in possession of this information every time the UCOs debriefed and mentioned this officer by name. The team, for its part, had no issue with that. Information gets held back for all sorts of valid reasons. It goes with the territory of covert policing. It is better to withhold certain information if it could affect your reaction and conduct on the plot in an adverse way. So the decision to withhold this officer's role from the UCOs was the right thing to do, but someone should have copied Colin Port into the script.

# CHAPTER 26

## The Cutting Room Floor

"The best laid schemes of mice and men
Go often askew," ¬ Robert Burns

Continuing in the vein of using the Truman Show analogy, we bring you some of the scenes left on the cutting room floor. The Operation George undercover officers, though professionals, were human and sometimes made mistakes. Some of them were potentially serious. Some also demonstrate the stresses of undercover work and others the behind-the-scenes humour, or a mix of the two.

## The Sherpa Hat

Neil, Robbie and Dave comprised the crew charged with most of the heavy lifting in the scams involving Jimmy. They knew their roles backwards when in Jimmy's company. The professional bond between those UCOs was as strong as any they had known, and they had worked undercover on many serious cases. They depended on each other, had each other's backs, trusted each other. They were tight. Off stage, in the privacy of the safe house, they were friends and those were the moments they could relax. They even felt at ease disagreeing with each other and leg-pulling was an art between them. The regular piss-takes were part of the glue holding them together as a unit. They never fell out and if there were any serious disagreements, they would hammer it out and then move on as one.

As a crew they switched that mental trigger as soon as they were about to go into action. They also hit the physical switches on their recording devices hidden somewhere on their bodies or in an item of clothing. *Game on*. The UCOs were now mindful of their casual conversations. Anything they said now could end up being disclosed to Jimmy and his defence team at some future point. All conversations from now would be in role and a minimum of chit chat took place.

A typical day began with a briefing in the holiday let used as a safe house. The cover team had rented for it for a couple of months in a small Devonshire village. Dave had turned up at the briefing in a jovial mood wearing what looked like a Sherpa hat. It was multi coloured with ear flaps and long tassels hanging off the flaps and a colour matched bobble on top. It's the sort of hat you might have seen Sherpa Tensing wearing, standing at the top of Everest posing for a photo with Edmund Hillary. There is a time and a place for everything, and Dave's choice of head gear was out of sync with the environment, climate and temperature. This was the sort of location that your elderly relatives went to for a couple of weeks in the summer, not where you would find a Sherpa in the local shop. The safe house was near to a small village shop full to the gunnels with everything you could imagine. The UCOs would often try to outdo each by mentioning something obscure that they were going to buy at this shop.

Back to the briefing, on entering the room the operational team briefing officers and the Cover Officer first looked at Dave and then at Neil and Robbie with an inquisitive glance and what seemed to be a disapproving tilt of the head. Robbie shook his head sideways as a signal before saying, "Okay, Dave. You can take the hat off now, mate. We've all seen it; you've made your statement."

Without a glance at Robbie, Dave just said, "What?"

Neil said, "The fucking stupid hat, we've all seen it. Now you can take it off."

Unfazed, Dave replied, "I'm going to the shop to get some milk and a MIG welder. Anyone want anything?" Everyone present laughed, used to Dave's idiosyncrasies. Dave made to walk out on his way to the shop.

Robbie called out after him, "Mate! Can you get me a Daily Mirror? If they haven't got the Mirror, get me anything." The team settled down. The kettle was on and Dave was fetching the milk.

The room filled with idle chatter until Dave's return.

Dave said loudly, "Robbie, they didn't have the Daily Mirror, so I got you this." He tossed a cold meat and potato pie towards Robbie.

Robbie smiled, saying, "Very funny, Dave. You're wasting your time on this job, you funny git."

"Well, you did say if they didn't have the Daily Mirror, get you anything. So, I had a look around the shop and got you a pie. What's the problem with that?" Dave said with a straight face.

More sarcastic comments and laughter at Robbie's expense. Dave felt chuffed with himself, and the stunt gave Robbie a cheesy grin every time their eyes met. Robbie just mouthed the word 'twat' back at him.

Neil and Robbie had agreed behind Dave's back not to make mention of his hat. They had decided he was wearing it to cause a stir and attract comment. Neither man was going to play into Dave's hands.

## PAG-IN-TON

After the briefing, the three men left in Robbie's car and made their way to Plymouth. Neil put a call to Jimmy and told him to be ready for a pickup at seven. On the way, Robbie stopped for fuel at a petrol station in the middle of nowhere. Neither Neil nor Dave made a move to assist in putting the fuel in or suggesting they would be going into pay. Robbie said in his best sarcastic tone, "I'll do it, lads, you just take it easy."

"Okay," said Dave.

As Robbie was just about to finish filling up Dave got out of the car with the map book in his hand and said to Robbie, "Get ready for this, mate." Robbie followed into the shop a few seconds behind Dave who was now talking to the attendant in an American accent.

Robbie heard Dave say, "Is this the road to Pag-in-ton? We're trying to get to Pag-in-ton." The attendant pushed his bottom lip over his top lip and moved his head left to right and in a strong Devon accent said, "I've never heard of it round here."

Dave, now getting louder and more animated, pointed left and right out the window and exaggerated his pronunciation. "Pag-in-ton, man." He then opened the map book and pointed at the town of Paignton. He continued, "Pag-in-ton."

The attendant chuckled at Dave's interpretation of the word Paignton and pointed out to the

'American' the English way of saying it, "It's pronounced Paynton."

Robbie was working hard to contain himself with Dave's performance. Dave was on top form with his wacky sense of humour starting with his Sherpa hat, Robbie's pie and his role as an American lost in the Dartmoor National Park.

## Lucky Robbie

Close to Jimmy's place, Dave put a call in to Jimmy telling him to be outside in five minutes. The three UCOs all reached for their recording devices and hit the on button. *Game on.* They had arranged to meet up with Jimmy and have a couple of drinks in Plymouth in and around the area of the flat (safe house). These social gatherings were always difficult to manage for the Plymouth team of UCOs. They knew they were exposing themselves to a defence team pulling any evidence apart because of the introduction of alcohol. Another concern was Jimmy driving home at the end of the evening. This concern was dealt with by one of the team, who on their way back into Plymouth would volunteer to pick Jimmy up at his house, thereby leaving his car at home, and a taxi was arranged to take him home. Job done, no chance of Jimmy drink driving.

As Robbie drove along, he saw Jimmy on the opposite side of the street from his house. The car pulled up and Jimmy jumped in the back next to Dave who greeted him with a string of insults and put downs about Jimmy's dress sense. Jimmy had the collar of his purple shirt over the collar of his black jacket. Robbie looked at Jimmy in the rear-view mirror. "You look like an Irish John Travolta." The usual volley of follow-ups filled the next five minutes. Robbie pulled up outside the pub and the other men got out and made their way into the pub. Robbie switched off his recording device, then drove the short distance to the flat to drop the car off. He put a short call into the Cover Officer to give him an update and told him they were looking at getting back to the flat around eleven.

Just before leaving the flat Robbie was aware that the micropore tape holding his device in place needed adjusting. After he had removed the device, he discovered that he didn't have any tape. He was frustrated by his oversight and took the chance of slipping it inside his sock. He tested it by walking up and down the stairs a few times. It seemed to be secure, so he activated the device then stuck it down his sock. Pulling up the sock, he set off for the pub.

As Robbie arrived, Jimmy stood up and headed for the bar to buy Robbie a pint. "Usual for you, Robbie, my man?"

"Yeah, cheers mate," Robbie said.

By the time Jimmy and Robbie had joined Neil and Dave at the table, those two were sitting with empty glasses. Robbie knew exactly what had occurred while Jimmy's back was turned. The two experienced UCOs had lost their drinks. The two partly drunk pints would now be on an empty table with an explanation ready if Jimmy asked any questions. Losing drinks was a tactic for avoiding going pint for pint. The group visited two or three of their favourite haunts, after which Neil invited the men to a curry at his expense. Everyone agreed, grateful for the offer, then followed Neil to the door with the UCOs leaving various amounts of beer in their glasses.

As they left, Dave put his arm around Jimmy's shoulder and playfully pulled him in towards him, still piss taking about his shirt and jacket. Stepping down from the pub doorway on to the pavement, a loud sound of metal landing on paving stone rang out. To Robbie, this sounded like Big Ben striking. He knew what it was. The device had worked its way out of the sock and had hit the pavement. The wire was still plugged in, and the bloody thing was being dragged along behind him.

Dave, still with an arm around Jimmy, continued without breaking step. Robbie, with lightning speed, dropped to one knee and within a split second the device was back in place. No harm done. Robbie knew how lucky he was. A schoolboy error: one that he would never repeat in his undercover career. The men had their curry at Neil's expense. Jimmy was put into a taxi and the three UCOs headed back to the flat. Dave had not finished his comedy show quite yet. He'd been on a roll all day, and this was his finale. The UCOs got back into the flat and deactivated their devices. A phone call was made to the Cover Officer to let him know the men were back in the flat safe and sound. He was able to tell the UCOs that Jimmy was back home and on the probe. Following routine, the tapes were marked as exhibits and together with the device secured in the flat until morning and debrief.

Once that routine was completed, the men sat around with a tin of beer and relaxed. Dave asked the group of UCOs, "Did anyone hear that fucking clunk as we left the last pub? It sounded like some wanker had dropped his recording device on the pavement in the company of the target. Then, I thought no one would be that stupid. Would they, Robbie? You cock."

Robbie, taking up the cudgel, said, "Mate, it couldn't have happened at a better time. As soon as it hit the pavement, I looked towards Jimmy and saw you had him in a hug and joking with him. It was like slow motion. I was down, grabbed the thing and shoved back in down my sock and back up again. That could have ended badly, to say the least. Doesn't bear thinking about, mate. I owe you one. Sorry lads. Fucking schoolboy error."

Neil, nonplussed by the event said, "No harm done, mate. You can buy the pies tomorrow. Good night, lads."

## The Kebab Shop

Working undercover on the plot for a long time brings its own burdens and stresses. On occasions when Jimmy wasn't with them, some of the UCOs let off steam. One such time involved Robbie and Dave who were close friends as well as colleagues.

One night they went out drinking together free from the presence of Jimmy Fulton. They relaxed and let their hair down because they are human. That's what people do. At the end of a heavy session, the pair ended up in a kebab shop. It's fair to say by the time they arrived there, slurred speech was the norm. They managed to place their orders but when Robbie got his, he told the man behind the counter it wasn't what he had ordered. An argument then broke out between Robbie and the Turkish guy who suddenly produced a huge, evil looking knife and started swinging it around in front of Robbie's face. Robbie, no doubt fearless in drink, got ready to fight but Dave stepped in to try to defuse the situation. Lucky for Robbie, Dave could handle himself having served in war zones in the employ of a foreign country. Robbie knew Dave was a real warrior who didn't talk or brag about his experiences. Dave, using his wits and common sense, decided the best course of action was to drag Robbie outside. Dave pulled him away from the blade and towards the shop door. Befuddled Robbie took objection and a push and pull session started between the two pals. The other Turks in the shop helped by calming down their knife-wielding compatriot so Dave and Robbie could get outside and on to the pavement. The trouble was Robbie still wanted a scrap. He offered Dave out, "Right fucking here and right fucking now!" You can imagine Robbie doing a passing imitation of a Hollywood drunk. He swayed from one foot to another which he probably thought was a fighting stance and continued baiting Dave. Dave's reaction was classic. He simply burst into fits of laughter on seeing his mate's antics. Robbie later realised Dave could have knocked seven bells out of him.

The last Robbie saw of Dave that night was his mate walking towards the flat (safe house) shouting his favourite phrase, "Fuck off! Wanker!" Robbie eventually crashed out in his own bed in the flat.

The next day in the Port O'Call café, tucking into a big boy's breakfast, they laughed and counted their blessings the local old bill hadn't been called. Had they got nicked they would have stayed in role in the police station and awaited the arrival of their brief or role-playing Cover Officer. Taking a nicking and bringing attention to themselves would have resulted in an immediate withdrawal from the plot.

## Roof Lining

Robbie drove a Range Rover Vogue, a decent car, to go with his image and legend of having a successful haulage company. He left the plot on one occasion to drive to his home. It was daylight when he set off, however it got dark later. Once it was past dusk and with his lights switched on, Robbie first noticed the interior light was flashing on and off at irregular intervals. His first thought was someone's lumped up his car (fitted a device to it). *Why would they do that?* he thought. Then he swore silently, *Twats*.

Pulling off the motorway at the first opportunity, he inspected the light fitting whilst giving a running commentary of what he was doing. He was convinced that someone was listening to him. "Right, you fuckers, wherever you are, I'm going to pull this car apart till I find your bug."

This was followed by "wankers," "twats" and "you piece of shit." He started trying to remove the plastic that covered the bulb. That didn't work. Then he forced the whole light fitting out of its housing in the roof lining. That didn't really help. So, he pulled down the roof lining. That did the trick and using the flame from a cigarette lighter, he saw into the space between the lining and the steel of the roof.

Robbie knew this car had been deployed on numerous jobs before Operation George and most likely had technical fits (listening/tracking/video) installed in it. That seems to be confirmed as he looked at a confusing mass of internal wiring stuck together with insulating tape. It was impossible for the untrained eye to tell if there was a current live technical fit. At that point, Robbie continued his monologue with the 'listening team' and called them all the names under the sun and decided to continue his journey home. Problem. He was unable to get the roof lining back into position. Only one thing for it. He drove home with the roof lining resting on his head. Every little bump in the road reminded him by the lining giving a gentle tap to his head.

On arriving home, Robbie went to remove his stuff from the boot. A Range Rover is a large hatchback and built in such a way that the rear window can also give access to the boot space. This was the moment he discovered that the rear window wasn't shut properly and had been tapping on the contact that switched the interior light on and off. The following day was spent putting the roof lining back in place and chuckling to himself, thinking about the soliloquy he'd delivered the previous night.

Then there was the incident of the missing pocket notebook which was as far removed from humour as anyone can imagine.

# CHAPTER 27

## Missing Notebook

Back to the heading of 'paranoia', another RUC officer loomed large in the Operation George saga. In what is believed to be the first and only time an RUC officer was despatched to the mainland to fire a police officer serving in one of the forty-three police forces in England and Wales, he arrived to officially inform one of the Plymouths UCOs his 'services were no longer required.' He was off Operation George for good. His 'crime' wasn't as nefarious as you might think.

The Plymouth team of UCOs had a safe house in Brixham. It was somewhere they could chill out without bumping into Tanya and Jimmy or any of their new friends and associates in Plymouth. They soon discovered there are four things to know about Brixham. It gets full of pensioners who arrive on coaches every day. That's a little surprising owing to the steep hills. The town sits across the bay from Torquay, which is livelier and in the UCOs' opinion, infinitely more desirable. But the Cover Officers were in control and sorted it out for them. The last thing to know is how the locals refer to Brixham. Depending on your employment seems to dictate how you refer to it. It's either Cow Town or Fish Town, and the two tribes of farmers and fishermen do not get on or indeed live in complete harmony together. Their relationship is like City and United or Celtic and Rangers. There is a fierce rivalry that spills over into punch-ups on a Friday and Saturday night after the old dears and their husbands have long gone. The farmers have their pubs and the fishermen have theirs.

There was one pub on the quayside that both sets would be attracted to because it was where the girls hung out. A fight broke out on one occasion in this pub where a massive bloke – he must have been a farmer because he would not have fitted into a fishing boat – threw a punch, sending his opponent flying horizontally and resulting in the poor guy landing on the far side of the room. The UCOs were unanimous in deciding this was a venue to be avoided at all costs. Instead, they chose to drink in a small local which just happened to be the first pub on leaving the safe house.

The UCOs invented a cover story as to why they were in Brixham. They put it about they were IT engineers employed by a London based company, working in and around Devon and parts of Cornwall. Robbie wasn't the savviest around IT so Dave told him to say that he did the 'ergonomics.' Robbie could hardly pronounce the word let alone spell it or know its meaning. Dave went on to explain, "Right, I'll say we do IT installations for a company based in London and we all have different parts of the business, and you do the ergonomics."

"Dave, mate, excuse my lack of knowledge but what the fuck does that word mean? It's best to stick to something I know and can talk about," Robbie said with genuine concern.

"Listen, all you have to say is you plan where the workstations, desks and cable runs go and that's it. Leave the rest to us," Dave assured him.

The safe house was about a five-minute walk up the hill from the quayside. It was someone's second home that was rented out as a holiday let to bring in an extra income stream out of season for the owner. The lads all had a room each which were off a first-floor landing. In the roof section above the landing was a Perspex domed skylight which gave an open, bright feeling to the landing. Sadly, it was also a resting place for huge seagulls to tap on at first light. The birds constant tap-tap-tap woke the team at dawn every morning, much to their annoyance. The landing window gave a great view across the bay to Torquay and the beautiful Victoria Hotel looking splendid in white. At this sight, they understood why Torquay is known as the English Riviera. The team sarcastically referred to their safehouse as the 'des-res' but were comforted when the Cover Officers often arranged briefings and debriefing at the Victoria Hotel. The UCOs ensured the complimentary bar was left empty on those occasions.

On one occasion, one undercover officer we shall call Mike was away for the day with Jimmy. The other team members were mooching around the town, which didn't take too long. It was a regular tactic for a Cover Officer to tag along out of sight of any UCO and Jimmy. Jimmy had dropped Mike off at the flat in Plymouth and he waited for Jimmy to clear the plot before setting off down to Brixham to join the other lads. The Cover Officer on this occasion, we will call him John, did the same, setting off about ten minutes before Mike. As John was nearing Brixham he called Neil to see where the team was as he fancied a quick half before retiring to his accommodation. Neil told him they were in their local and John agreed to meet them there. After about ten minutes, John walked into the bar and joined the team of IT Engineers. Dave soon got the conversation round to ergonomics and taking the piss out of Robbie and how he'd made a gigantic cockup on the job that day. It was all cock and bull, but it served a purpose if anyone was earwigging the conversation. Within ten minutes of John arriving, Neil got a call from Mike asking where they were. Neil told him they were in the pub and Mike agreed to join them there. At that point, the UCOs present in the pub had no inkling of any untoward issues. But alarm bells started to ring in John's head.

Mike walked into the pub and joined the team. John quietly asked Mike if he had completed his work, gesturing writing on his hand with a pen: code for have you done your notes? Mike answered in the affirmative, but John was unconvinced, though he held off, probably believing this wasn't the time or place to hold an inquisition. John left the company, and the remainder of the evening followed the usual pattern – beer quaffed followed by either a sit-down meal or fish and chips from the local chippy. Robbie had to be up early the next day to meet up with John at the Gordano Service Station on the M5 motorway. They planned to go into Bristol to look for a lock up. Just as Robbie was turning in for the night, Mike asked if he could come along in the morning just for something to do.

"If it's okay with John, it's okay with me. I'm off at 7:30ish," Robbie said.

"Fine, I'll speak to John and see you in the morning," Mike said.

The following morning arrived with Robbie up and ready to go, looking forward to a full English at the motorway services or a nice greasy spoon cafe in Bristol. He knocked on Mike's door and discovered Mike fast asleep. Robbie shouted out that he was going now. Mike mumbled, "Okay, I'll come up in my car and meet you at the services."

Robbie drove the hundred-mile journey to the service station, a journey of about two hours for him but just over the hour for Dave, Devon and Cornwall's most wanted road hog. Robbie and John met up and made their way to the self-service café. They decided to give the rubber-like egg and cold sausage a miss and elected for the Bristol greasy spoon option. Robbie told John Mike was about ten minutes away so they should wait there for him. John looked surprised and said he didn't know Mike was coming. That was when Robbie informed John about the earlier conversations he'd had with Mike. Robbie had no idea anything was out of place, but he sensed John was wondering what the hell was going on.

Robbie called Mike to find out where he was and to tell him two guys were waiting on him at Gordano, and they were starving. Mike told him he was stuck in traffic on the motorway, but he could see the motorway one-mile advance sign for the services. Robbie and John were able to see the motorway traffic and noted there weren't any delays or hold ups. At that, John phoned Mike and told him to meet them in the first layby as he exited the M5 at Junction 19. The plan was to leave two cars there and all three of them would continue into Bristol in one motor.

John and Robbie made their way to the large layby and waited for Mike. After some delay, Mike called John to say he'd missed the exit and would have to continue to the next one at

Junction 18 which was on the other side of the major road works to the bridge over the River Avon. These road works always caused delays, but this was a Saturday morning, and the traffic was light. The UCO and the Cover Officer waited in silence for the most part. John was obviously working through things surrounding Mike's recent performance.

Robbie was just plain hungry and regretted agreeing to have Mike come along. Then like something out of a Disney cartoon a Black BMW approached, steam coming from the bonnet; it was travelling at best ten miles per hour. The front wheels were splayed and out of line with the front wings. Every panel was damaged including the roof, and there was no windscreen. Had it not been for recognising Mike behind the wheel aiming the wreck towards them, neither of the guys would have thought it was the nice shiny black beamer that was once in apple pie condition.

Shrugging, Mike got out of the wreck and looked and acted totally nonchalant. He offered an opinion it wasn't as bad as it looked. He was utterly unfazed, unlike John who fired off a barrage of questions, "Mate what in fuck's name? Have you driven that down the motorway like that? What's happened?"

Mike began to tell his tale of woe. He'd come off at Junction 18 and exited the roundabout to head back towards Junction 19. As he was about to head west on the main carriage way, a fox ran across the slip road. He hit the brakes and turned the steering wheel to avoid the quick brown fox and went down the embankment, rolling over and ending up back on the wheels. A lorry driver stopped and pulled him out with a tow rope that he just happened to have. Once on the slip road, he started the engine and drove along the hard shoulder to meet up at the layby. Robbie, listening with incredulity, thought, *What a load of shite! This is for John to sort out, it doesn't involve me and a lock-up is still to be found.* This was the last time Robbie saw Mike. Robbie continued into Bristol and stopped at the first place that sold hot food, after which he went into Bristol and secured a lock-up in the form of a 'To Rent' private domestic garage advertised in a newsagent's window. It was in a block of garages behind a high-rise tower block in a working-class area of Bristol. The lock-up was ideal for a future plan involving Jimmy and a dodgy motor.

Meanwhile, John and Mike had to arrange for a local recovery company that would be prepared to recover the beat-up BMW back to a secure police workshop in London. Once the BMW was being piggy backed to London, Mike and John headed back to Plymouth to meet up with the operational team members and give them a full debrief on the events. It was during this question-and-answer session that the subject of Mike's pocket notebook (PNB) arose. The PNBs were always left with the Cover Officer or ops team or secure in the safe house. It never went onto the plot. Mike claimed his book was safe and secure in his hiding place in the safe house in Brixham. The team in Brixham were called and directed to the hiding place and asked to retrieve Mike's PNB. The safe house was searched top to bottom with a negative result, as was the Plymouth flat which was searched by Mike and John.

Mike then said it may have been in the crashed BMW which by now was in a secure police garage in London. A member from the London

Undercover Office was called out to gain access to the garage and search the BMW inside out. Once more, no PNB. Mike then admitted he had it in his holdall when he went to a public gym in Plymouth a day or so ago. Things now were serious. The UCOs, including Robbie, were all together in the safe house in Brixham. John called them to offer a quick explanation of the day's events. He also instructed them not to return to Plymouth under any circumstance and not to take any calls from Jimmy. What is more, he instructed them to return to their home addresses and stay there until contacted.

A sombre atmosphere fell over the team of UCOs. *What if someone found it?* They knew the whole job could now be destroyed by one of their own. Anyone could be in possession of that PNB. *What if it found its way into the hands of a local hack reporter? What if it was in the hands of a real Plymouth criminal? What if Jimmy had it?* That's a lot of 'what ifs,' but any of those could have proved fatal in more ways than one.

Just like a starburst, the UCOs from Brixham headed off in the directions of their homes in this cloud of uncertainty. They had all agreed to keep in contact with each other using their personal mobiles so that they could report on any contact made by Jimmy. They could also keep in the loop about any updates from the cover and operational teams or discuss between themselves any suggested course of action for the teams. Independently from each other, the undercover officers started to mull things over as they drove in different directions. These were ultra-smart guys that could nit-pick the bones out of a series of events and dialogue. They had been told that the PNB may have been lost for a few days when Mike said he had it in his hold all in Plymouth gym. They knew that alone was a cardinal sin, punishable with the sack. *What was he thinking, taking it there? It was placing his colleagues in danger. There wasn't sufficient time so how could Mike have completed his notes before joining the team in the pub on the previous night. Lying to the Cover and his colleagues to cover up his fuck-up; how could these men trust him again? Simple and short answer to that question was, never.*

In this line of work, when you are in a team behind the lines you depend and trust on the guy or gal next to you to do their part. Mike, at worst, had knowingly put these guys in real danger. At best, he had done it unwittingly. His colleagues had families, children, wives, brothers, sisters, loved ones. *Unforgivable*. A thousand questions and scenarios ran across the minds of the undercover team as they drove in different directions to the safety of their homes and families. The one comforting thought was there was no connection between Plymouth, Jimmy or Mike that would lead anyone to their front door. This responsibility ultimately was in the hands of the individual officers. Each knew a sterile corridor was in place that stopped any contamination from their murky undercover lives spilling over into their peaceful home and family lives.

Once home, the team called John to let him know they had arrived safe and sound. Neil, Dave and Robbie all rang each other and slagged Mike off. They agreed never to work with him again. As far as they were concerned,

Mike was now *persona non grata.* What is more, all agreed that status should be recorded in the Undercover Officers National Index. They strongly felt Mike was finished as a UCO. *Good riddance to bad rubbish*, they thought.

Another point that the three undercover officers raised with each other was the amount of detail Mike wrote in his notes. We have briefly mentioned previously the danger of writing too much detail and copious notes. It's a car crash waiting to happen. Not normally because some wanker has lost his PNB, but it gives the defence team at any future trial a massive area to attack an officer's evidence. The contemporaneous record of any conversation is the recording: the tape. Officers who write too much detail into their notes can often contradict the tape recording, perhaps unwittingly. This potentially leads to an uncomfortable cross examination, an experience to be avoided at all costs. The undercovers, the operational and cover team had all sat in debriefings when the UCOs read notes from their PNBs. The PNB is an 'Aide Memoire' and should be written up in that style. If, during a debrief, the topic is about a direct conversation, an address or a phone number and it cannot be recalled, it's best practice to inform the debriefing officer it's on the tape and they can retrieve the exact detail there. However, Mike wrote buckets full of information in his notes. Names, addresses, phone numbers, vehicle registrations, everything went in there. Poor tradecraft and bad practice and unnecessary. That was why the loss of his PNB was such a disaster and caused such an alarm.

The next day was a busy time for everyone involved in Operation George – the listeners, enquiry teams, and those monitoring trackers. Both the ops team and Cover Officers were still on the plot. Jimmy was alone in Plymouth without the undercover team available to step in should he decide to go independent on some scheme. Speed was required to resolve the situation.

The cover team contacted each individual UCO at their homes and told them that the situation had been risk assessed. Mike had informed them that the book did not contain any information that could lead a third party to the Plymouth operation. He added there was nothing in his notes that could compromise the op. Neil, Dave and Robbie knew that was bollocks and told them it was more of Mike's lies and bullshit. They wanted a full risk assessment carried out by Colin Port or his nominated officer before going back on the plot.

They strongly felt this was not an event that could be swept under the carpet to avoid embarrassing someone. All three UCOs refused to redeploy until their condition was met. As a result, a senior RUC officer arrived from Belfast to conduct an internal investigation into the loss of the PNB and a further risk assessment. He was satisfied from probe product that Jimmy had no knowledge and his movements and behaviour had not changed. The decision to redeploy was conveyed to the three undercover officers. All three men were asked if they were happy to return to Plymouth. All three said yes. The operation was back on. Mike was never seen or heard of again.

# CHAPTER 28

## The Voice

The Plymouth team had been operating for a long time by the time of Fulton's arrest, and prior to that day it was business as usual, trying to dream up more schemes and scams to enable them to be close to their target; close enough for several hours a day to let him talk and record those conversations. Dave professed to know more about IT than any of the other UCOs, so it fell to him to propose a scam involving the theft of high-value computer microchips. Luckily for him, one of the Cover Officers knew his computer onions and backed him.

"Didn't know they were made in the UK," Robbie said sceptically.

The Cover Officer wised him up. "Most aren't. They are imported from Asia and the States."

"What about the buyers? Who would buy this stuff? More to the point, what do we tell Jimmy?" Robbie queried.

"There's lots of smaller outfits busy making high end gaming computers. They are the customers as the chips are the most expensive components," Dave added.

"That might work, as I don't think Jimmy knows the difference between a microchip and a potato chip unless it's got McCains on the packet," Robbie said.

"We could say the same about you, Robbie," someone at the back of the room said.

With the plan now sanctioned, Neil arranged for a meeting of the Plymouth firm at the Weston-

Super-Mare lockup, which was still wired for sound. Naturally, Jimmy was present as a valued and trusted member of the criminal gang. During this two-hour long planning meeting, all present were unaware persons other than the regular listeners were eavesdropping. They included teams of detectives gathered in preparation for interviewing Fulton and others following their arrests.

Preparing for the end of the operation, Colin Port's team trawled the UK mainland for a team of top detectives to conduct the interviews of Jimmy and his crew. This expedition was conducted by the Special Branch departments of the forty-three geographical police areas in England and Wales. What were the chances of members of the interview teams knowing any of the Operation George UCOs?

Once the interviewing team had been identified it was called to a secret briefing at Colin Port's clandestine operation base on the UK mainland. That briefing was to last over several days. Starting with an overall picture of what Operational George entailed, the assembled detectives were broken down into individual interviewing teams of two. Each team was then given many hours of covert recorded conversations between the UCOs and a target. These conversations, known as product, were all the conversations captured on listening probes in the homes of Fulton and Gibson and Fulton's Renault Laguna. Additionally, there were many hours of covertly recorded conversations captured by the UCOs using hidden recording devices. Within them were the admissions used as evidence to convict Jimmy and his crew in court.

As any seasoned detectives of certain eras know, at any gathering of the 'old school detectives' a natural bonding process begins or is fostered, usually by way of late nights in the bar or sometimes early evenings in the bar followed by curry and then a late night in the bar. This is when the 'war stories' get trotted out: "Do you know such and such? He/she was on my CID course," or "I was giving evidence in number one court at the Bailey," or "When I was on the RCS." The latter is the 'When-I's' favourite. They are known for prefacing every war story with, "When I…"

Two of the detectives selected for this job were two top Johnnys from one of the UK's finest, Clive and Pete, we will call them. Both were highly respected by colleagues no matter what rank. At the risk of sounding controversial in an age of political correctness within the modern police service, they were two modern day detectives who were versed in the more acceptable old school methods and tactics but allied to a complete knowledge of PACE to enable successful interviews resulting in convictions. These guys were comfortable with the task they had been handed and tackled it with the same professional attitude and approach as every other job, big or small. Clive and Pete mixed in well with the other team members and threw themselves into the social gatherings with gusto.

On the second day of the briefing, the teams were gathered, poring over transcripts, making notes, exchanging ideas and strategies, and asking searching questions of the full-time members of the operation team. During one of these sessions one of the listeners came in and announced, "If you guys are interested there is a meeting involving the UCOs and Jimmy taking place in a warehouse in the West Country right now. The boss said you guys can give your ears a treat if you fancy it."

Clive and Pete were on the move before the fella had finished his invitation. Like two thoroughbred racehorses at the start of the big race, they were at the head of the field making the early running with the listening room as their winning post. The new arrivals settled down where they were able. Standing in complete silence, they tuned their ears into the voices emanating from a set of small speakers on a desk. The UCOs and Jimmy were in the warehouse discussing a bit of work that was coming up. Neil was delegating who was going to do what. There was the usual banter between the group, which the interviewing teams interpreted as a relaxed atmosphere and not at all what they expected. But those present who had experienced undercover operations before or had past dealings with similar product knew, contrary to common belief, that all UCOs didn't talk out of the corners of their months, effing and blinding like some Cockney flash Harry.

Clive and Pete listened carefully, staring at the two speakers on the desk as an aid to concentration, when simultaneously they looked into each other's eyes. Not uttering a word, they thought the same thing at the same time, *Fuck me!* Both had recognised one of the voices as one of their own. Clive, Pete and the UCO had all been part of the same shift back on division, in uniform and on CID. As always, both maintained their professionalism, said nothing and maintained their composure. Both made a mental note to speak with each other later away from anyone else.

Before dinner that day while taking a stroll around the sports field, Clive and Pete discussed the situation. They agreed not mentioning it in the listening room was the right thing to do. Their silence effectively protected the UCO being identified. They also agreed to keep the facts to themselves and not share this with anyone at the briefing location. They believed the right thing to do was contact the Special Branch (SB) Detective Inspector (DI) in their own force who had nominated them for Colin Port's interviewing teams. He listened to what they had to say, expressing he had no clue of any of the identities of the UCOs deployed on Operation George. Unfazed by this account, he reassured Clive and Pete he would call the operational team to appraise them of this development. Content they had contacted the SB DI, Clive and Pete went for dinner. After dinner, the two guys sat in Clive's room enjoying a glass of red wine that Clive always seem to have available. They recounted the very second each of them recognised the voice of their old mate and described each other's facial expressions. Naturally, they could not reach agreement as to which of the two was more composed on hearing the UCO in the listening room. They did agree their old mate was buying the first round when this thing was all over. Clive had the last word. "The fucking exxies [expenses] he's on, that's a given, Pete." After the glass of wine, they sauntered into the bar to have a few pints with the rest of the interviewing teams and contact home using their mobile phones. After a quick chat with their respective wives, Clive's phone pinged. It was a text from the SB DI asking them to attend the ops team's office at 08:15 the next morning to see the boss. He clarified he had not disclosed their friend's alias nor anything else about him. He signed off the text with: *Please acknowledge by text. Regards. Denis.*

Clive read the text and replied with: *'ok ta guv'* and put the phone back in his pocket.

Exercising oodles of discretion owing to the presence of too many others, Clive decided to wait to inform Pete of the text. Both were aware the normal working day started at nine in the morning so later that night and showing the text to Pete, he said, "Okay, we had better make up a cover story just in case these nosey bastards see us going across early."

Pete said, "We'll tell them we wanted to get away a bit sharpish tomorrow for a commitment back on Division."

They agreed that they would only refer to the UCO as 'the voice' and not even identify him by his alias. Come the following morning, the two men walked the short distance from the accommodation block across to the office. They found the boss's door open, and he beckoned the two men to enter with a wave of the hand. The boss asked Pete to close the door. The entire story was pored over with the boss agreeing completely with their decision making and the steps they had taken. He fully understood. The boss asked the two officers if they were still happy to be part of the team and no inference would be drawn by him if they felt too close and would rather step down. Both detectives glanced towards each other and without hesitation turned back to the boss and said in unison, "I'm in."

The boss smiled at their double act and said, "Thank you. I think you two will be valuable members of this team. I can only hope the other guys are as switched on and as savvy as you two guys." Some light-hearted chatter followed, mainly about their reaction to recognising the voice and referring to their friend only as 'the voice'.

As Clive and Pete were leaving the office, Clive mentioned their cover story concocted to mask this visit. The boss, without looking up from his desk, shook his head from side to side before saying, "You guys think of everything, get out of here."

Clive and Pete returned to their force the next day and waited for the call to return for a final briefing and allocation of interviews. The UCO got the heads up on the voice recognition episode and parked it in the 'no worries tray.'

He knew the two detectives well and had no concerns whatsoever about their integrity nor his identity and safety being compromised.

Months later, following the completion of all the interviews and after Fulton and Gibson had been charged, Clive and Pete returned to their usual daily routine back on Division. Clive was walking through the rear yard of a nick heading for the car park when he saw the UCO, 'the voice', walking towards him. They nodded to each other, but the UCO was sporting a cheeky little smile. Clive, however, after the nod of the head sheepishly dropped his eyes and did not see the smile. Still approaching, the UCO spoke, "It's okay, mate. I heard what happened and how you dealt with it."

"Thanks," Clive replied still a tad bashful. But then recovered his composure, saying, "My pleasure, you owe me wine, lots of wine. You almost stopped my heart when I heard your voice. Good job, by the way."

They both continued walking in opposite directions, the UCO heading for the police station building. He found Pete sitting in the canteen drinking tea and reading a report. The UCO approached him from behind to surprise him. Just as Pete raised the mug of tea to his lips the UCO said, " Have you been listening in to my fucking conversation?"

Once more recognising 'the voice', Pete remained statue-like and without turning around, he said, "Half of the UK police have been listening in to your fucking conversation." Then turning towards the UCO, he stood slowly, turning his face towards his mate, beaming a huge smile and offering a man hug.

"What the fuck! Get your paws off me," the UCO exclaimed.

"Mate, you owe me and Clive dinner and beers but vino in Clive's case. Are you okay? That was some bit of work you were on."

The UCO strolled off to get two more cups of tea and they continued talking about their different experiences on Operation George. Pete was amazed how they, the UCOs, had managed to keep the illusion going for so long. Following this encounter, there were always conspiratorial nods and winks passed between them with Pete or Clive often asking, "Where's my fucking dinner?" On occasions it would be a jovial inquiry asking the UCO if he had been down to the warehouse lately. The UCOs deployed on George came from all over the UK, as did the interview teams. What are the odds of the interviewing teams knowing the UCOs? Perhaps as high as a million to one.

# CHAPTER 29

## The Strike

Despite the stumbles and some disharmony in the Plymouth undercover team, activities continued on a professional level. However, there could be no doubt some pressure was being put on Colin Port to bring down the final curtain on the *Truman Show*. It was obviously costing bundles to finance and Port possibly had eyes on legal issues such as an allegation of abuse of process. He would have also assessed what new stuff was coming out of Jimmy and the stresses, strains and mental conditions of the gang of three in Plymouth – Neil, Dave and Robbie. Those three did all the heavy lifting when it came to occupying and controlling Jimmy.

Some friction had started to develop between those three and some of the Cover Officers. This had also been noticed by the operational team, that's to say the team based away from Plymouth who oversaw the operations in Plymouth and Cornwall, reporting directly to Colin Port in Belfast. That team was responsible for briefing and debriefing both Operation George teams, including the UCOs and the Cover Officers. To the credit of the operational team, its practice was not to become involved in the disagreements but to leave the UCOs and Cover Officers to sort it out between themselves. The imminent arrest of Jimmy Fulton was perhaps timely.

On Monday, 11 June 2001, the evening before his arrest, Neil, Dave and Robbie, together with

Jimmy, were having a quick drink in a pub just up from Jimmy's Plymouth house. The house was part of a large estate to the north of the city centre. By now, Jimmy's wife and kids were also living with him. There was no off-road parking on the estate and trying to find a parking spot was always a hassle as they were at a premium. However, Jimmy had managed to find a spot directly opposite his lounge window but on the opposite side of the road from his house.

Earlier, Robbie had travelled with Jimmy, and they met with Neil and Dave in the pub on the estate. Robbie planned to get a lift back with the other two UCOs. All four had been in the pub for five minutes or so when Robbie's mobile phone rang. It was the Cover Officer using the cryptic coded question, "Are you all right to talk?"

Robbie, following protocols and his training, said, "Yeah mate, everything go all right with that load?" He often used words and phrases that a third party would associate with haulage. That was his back story with Jimmy, that he had a haulage company that was a part front to launder his criminal proceeds. Jimmy was by now used to Robbie receiving such calls and walking away from the group. Once alone out on the pub car park, Robbie was able to continue the conversation, ensuring Jimmy remained in view to prevent the target catching him unawares and possibly hearing something he should not.

Confident he was alone, Robbie told the Cover Officer to go ahead.

"I've had a request from the operational team, so don't shoot the messenger."

"What the fuck is it now?" Robbie said.

"The firearms team have asked that the car is parked the other way round so that the driver's door opens into the road. As it is, the driver's door is kerbside, they want him to turn it around."

Words dripping with more than a little irony, Robbie said, "No worries. I'll explain it to Jimmy, I'm sure he'll understand. Do they want Jimmy to wear a Hi-Vis vest in the morning so they know it's him, mate?"

Following a little more banter, Robbie agreed to sort it out, but he wasn't yet sure how. He walked back into the pub and joined the group. Neil played his part by saying, "Everything okay with that load, Robbie?"

Quick thinking as ever, Robbie said, "Yeah, no worries mate. I need to make a phone call from a box. Jimmy, can I borrow your car?"

In private thoughts, Robbie guessed the armed arrest team boss had taken a drive past to get an accurate mental picture of the scene, so he was able put his arrest plan together.

Unhesitating, Jimmy replied, "No worries, my man, here you go," as he tossed over the Laguna keys.

Robbie walked the short distance to Jimmy's house and was engrossed by some troubling thoughts. Parking spots are like rocking horse shit in this street so the chances of me getting the same spot is a million to one shot. The new parking spot might not suit the firearms boys and we could be playing this musical car game all fucking night.

On reaching the car, he had another thought – Tanya's indoors, so I'd better make this look real. No use just moving it in case Tanya spots me. I'd better make this good as it's the finale and I don't want to fuck it all up.

With these thoughts battering his brain cells, Robbie drove off in the direction of the phone box he knew on the estate. He went as far as going into the phone box and making an imaginary call just in case one of Jimmy's neighbours saw his car with a stranger sitting in it outside a phone box. After five minutes, Robbie got back in the car and drove back to find a parking place near Jimmy's house. Not for the first time, Robbie thought, *Well, the gods are smiling on me.* As he approached the spot where Jimmy's car had been parked, he saw it was already taken. But then the car directly in front pulled out, leaving the perfect spot for him to park Jimmy's car afresh. *Job done*, he thought.

As he was locking the car door, Robbie was startled to hear that that distinctive Northern Ireland accent call out, "Tell that man of mine to get home. His tea's on the table." It was Tanya. Robbie gave a cheery wave in acknowledgement that he would pass on the message to Jimmy. With that, he walked back to the pub and re-joined his mates.

Handing Jimmy his keys, Robbie reassured Neil with, "All sorted, Neil, no worries. Jimmy, I saw Tanya and she says your tea's on the table." Robbie and Neil could not help thinking, *I'm glad it wasn't one of Jimmy's 'invitations to tea.'* The get together in the pub ended with all three UCOs leaving and Jimmy walking home for his tea – the last time he'd be eating tea with his family for a long time. Before the parting of the ways, arrangements were made for Jimmy to pick Robbie up from the flat at 6:30 the following morning, Tuesday 12 June 2001. Neil and Robbie knew it was a fifteen-minute drive from Jimmy's house to the flat so he would be leaving his place at around 6:15 am. That would be the time his whole world would fall around his ears, and he would start to pay for his crimes. The vehicle had a remote-controlled immobiliser fitted so the firearms boys could allow him to get inside the car and then hit the immobiliser. Jimmy would be trapped and under control in a car that wasn't going anywhere. Checkmate Jimmy Fulton!

The UCOs went back to the flat, packed up their personal kit, loaded their cars and drove out of the square for the last time and into the sunset. It made absolute common sense for them to get out of town just in case something went wrong. In the event something did, there were always the phones to contact Jimmy if they needed to call him or if he decided to go out that night with or without the car. There were a few possible permutations: likely or unlikely events. Nothing ever goes to plan. They say in battle the game play goes out the window as soon as the first round is fired. Fortunately, everything went to plan. The long-time target, Jimmy Fulton, was arrested in a dawn swoop by armed officers of the Devon and Cornwall Constabulary. He was driven a few miles to a nearby airfield where a military helicopter awaited. Soon after take-off, he was locked up in a Northern Ireland holding centre to await questioning.

Safe in that knowledge, the UCOs and the Cover Officers drove to Exeter on the evening of the day of Jimmy Fulton's arrest. Hotel rooms were booked, and they went out for a meal together. They don't recall giving Jimmy much thought and the mood was more a relief it was over than of celebration. They knew as seasoned professionals it was the end of an amazing 'bit of work.'

# CHAPTER 30

## Interviews

The RUC interview team dedicated to William Fulton, known as Jimmy, had prepared their strategy, structure and staged disclosure for months. No stone would remain unturned. These diligent detectives would do their best to ensure as many victims and the families of those victims as possible would have their day in court. Jimmy had killed, maimed, terrorised and ruled his corner of Northern Ireland with fear and savage violence. Not any more, Jimmy, son. Your time is over. Make way for the rule of law.

This was the mantra of two experienced detectives we will call Detective Inspector Eddie Roche and Detective Sergeant Dennis O'Brien. They were close friends as well as colleagues. The two men worked from an office within shouting distance of the Stormont Parliament Buildings in Belfast. On their desks lay files of unsolved open cases ranging from murder, kidnapping, bombings, robbery, drug dealing and punishment shootings. Jimmy Fulton's blood-stained dabs were now all over them. Not as a result of a tout, victim or an eyewitness but by Jimmy himself. Self-confessed involvement. Eddie and Dennis already had Jimmy's confessions; the interviews were almost a formality.

The day of reckoning had finally arrived. Eddie and Dennis watched from the window of the Special Branch (SB) Office at Belfast Airport as the military helicopter touched down a short distance away from them. The chopper's rotors stopped, and the engine fell silent. From the opened door stepped a guy in military dress wearing an aircrew helmet, followed by an RUC policer officer colleague dressed in a suit. Then came Jimmy dressed in jeans and a polo shirt, instantly recognised by the two detectives from interviews, posters and mug shots around the SB Offices in the province. Eddie and Dennis knew that Fulton wasn't getting off the hook this time. He was oven ready, and the oven was at the right temperature to slide him in and watch him cook in his own juices. "Mr William James Fulton you are well and truly fucked this time," whispered Eddie.

There was the normal custody procedure to follow so the two detectives waited to get the ball rolling with their interview strategy. It was agreed at SIO level that the disclosure would be staged. Interview one would be focused on dates and events. Two would be further detail around those dates and events. Three would be associations. Four would be when Eddie and Dennis pulled the pin out of the hand grenade and monitored Fulton's reaction. Stage four was the disclosure that his best friends on the mainland were undercover cops and they had covertly recorded every conversation he had with them.

The moment finally arrived when Eddie and Dennis signed the custody record, taking charge of Fulton in the presence of his solicitor, and walked him to the interview room. The four men sat around a table and Dennis pushed the record button on the wall mounted recording machine. After the prolonged buzzing sound

Eddie made the customary introductions which included asking Fulton to state his name. Looking at Fulton, Eddie invited him to introduce himself. "Would you please state your name for the tape, please."

Fulton remained silent with his eyes fixed on a stain in the paintwork above the heads of Eddie and Dennis. Fulton was exercising his anti-interrogation techniques. He was taking himself mentally out of the room and focusing on anything and everything other than the two officers and their questions. This silence and anti-interrogation methods continued through the next two interviews, but the officers stuck to their planned structure and questions. The staged interviews and questioning zeroed in towards the moment the detectives were to deliver the knockout punch.

Interview four followed along the lines of the previous three. On this occasion, Fulton was attempting to balance his chair on two legs. He had his fingertips on the end of the table, his feet raised off the floor and trying to find the point of balance where he could remove his fingertips and hold his position in the chair without support. In no rush to spoil Fulton's day and piss all over his fireworks, the two officers stuck to the plan. Eddie took the pin out and threw the grenade onto the table right under Fulton's nose.

Eddie fixed his eyes on Fulton and expressing no emotion said, "Your associates on the mainland. Your friends, Neil, Dave, Robbie, Gary, Hands, they are all undercover police officers and have been covertly recording all your conversations with them." That got his attention. Fulton's face expressed his thoughts – *What did he just fucking say?*

Fulton's face wore a glum expression as he set the chair down on all four legs and looked directly into Eddie's eyes. "That's right, all cops like me and Dennis. Cops that had you talking for hours and hours and hours about your involvement in countless crimes from murder to drug dealing," Eddie said, and then in a subdued tone of triumph, added, "I imagine you would like to have a consultation in private with your solicitor now. Interview concluded."

Dennis reached across and pressed the stop button on the recording device. The tape labels were completed in deadly silence. You could have heard a pin drop in the room. Fulton was first to his feet and keen to get out of the room. His world had just collapsed. He must have thought, *What the fuck have I said? What do they know?* The answer was simple, one word. Everything.

Eddie and Dennis escorted Fulton and his solicitor back to the custody staff. They guessed it would be some time before Fulton and his solicitor would be ready for the next interview. The two friends put an arm around each other's shoulder. Eddie pulled Dennis into him as if they had just won the Champions League Final with a late goal and said, "Take that, you fucker."

The two detectives walked into the SB office and were surprised to find so many of their colleagues still sitting at their desks. Tim, a short bald detective, couldn't contain himself. He shouted across at the interviewing officers. "How did it go, boss? What did he do when you told him about the boys on the mainland?"

Dennis got in first. "He shite his pants right there in front of us. I kid you not. Shite himself."

"You're joking me, come on. Did he really?" asked Tim.

The office broke out in hand clapping, cheers, back slapping and laughter. They had Fulton on the hook and he was going nowhere… except prison for a long time.

Much later and after her son's arrest whilst Fulton was on remand, his mum was picked up on a mic while visiting Jimmy in jail. She was heard asking Jimmy, "Is that nice man Robbie a policeman?"

Jimmy replied, "Yes, Mother, even that nice man Robbie. And stop calling him Robbie, it's not his real name. He and the others all used false names and were undercover policemen."

But it wasn't quite over yet – there were legal battles ahead.

# CHAPTER 31

## Bail

Before the legal battles proper were enjoined, Fulton's defence team won an early skirmish in that they successfully applied for bail in the wake of his brother, Mark 'Swinger' Fulton committing suicide in his Northern Ireland prison cell. He was granted bail so he could attend his brother's funeral. Such a bail hearing would have taken place in front of a single judge in private with both defence and prosecution arguing their respective cases. It is highly likely the defence argued that the whole case against Jim Fulton would collapse if the covertly recorded admissions were to be ruled inadmissible. The prosecution probably agreed because that scenario was true. So, with conditions, Fulton was bailed.

Later, Robbie was on holiday in the South of France. It was his habit to always take the whole month of August off. He had set off with his children with a caravan in tow. The idea was to spend about two weeks travelling to the *Cote d'Azur* and back again. Avoiding motorways, he would take the scenic route through northern France, across into Germany, Austria, Switzerland, Italy, Monaco and back into France, meeting his wife at Nice Airport for a two week stay at a camp site.

Relaxing at the camp site, Robbie received a call on his job mobile. At any one time, he may have had several mobile phones with him: personal, his job mobile, his legend mobile and a phone for any UC job he may be involved with. It was one of the Plymouth Cover Officers, the one who had planned the Lowry painting scam.

"Can you talk?" she asked, using the usual code phrase.

Robbie thought, Fuck, what's happened? She knows I'm on holiday and out of the country because of the ring tone. Do I need to get back to the UK for a court case? Has a job gone tits up and I need to get back in there to protect an informant? What is it?!

"Yeah, I'm okay to talk."

"I have some bad news for you," she said, adding swiftly, "Jimmy's has been released on bail."

All Robbie could say was, "What the fuck are you doing phoning me up to tell me that?"

It was a brief call. Robbie undertook a brief self-risk assessment (and risk to his family) and concluded there was nothing he could do about it and the chances of Fulton coming on his holidays to the same site was a one in a billion chance. He told no one and got on with the rest of his holiday.

But a scare was to come just a few days after this call. The family visited a different camp site to use their facilities on a day basis. The sunbeds were set up by the pool when the blood in Robbie's veins ran ice cold. He was relaxing, eyes half shut, when he heard people arriving behind them to set themselves up. Startled, he heard the adult voice of a male speaking in that unmistakable Northern Irish accent. *Fucking no way!* he thought. Positioning his head to get a look at the fella, he saw he was tattooed, had cropped hair and aged about the same as Jimmy Fulton. His heart skipped a beat at the sight before he convinced himself it wasn't him despite an uncanny likeness. *How spooky is that?* he thought. Robbie could see this guy had all the trademarks of a paramilitary and he was sure if he'd asked him if he knew Jimmy Fulton he would have said, 'Yes.' Robbie had met both Fulton brothers and had been shown photographs of Billy Wright – the top echelon of the LVF and knew how similar they looked. Considering his family's welfare and that of his own, they left for the safety of their own camp site and never returned to the scene of the scare.

# CHAPTER 32

# Belfast

Finally, the trial of The Queen v William James Fulton was scheduled to take place at Belfast Crown Court. It was held with no jury present under the Diplock courts arrangements for Northern Ireland. Diplock courts were criminal courts in Northern Ireland for non-jury trial of specified serious crimes used for political and terrorism-related cases during and after the Troubles. They were abolished by legislation introduced in 2007. However, non-jury trial remains possible in Northern Ireland on a case-by-case certification basis rather than automatically applying to scheduled offences.

Robbie was warned to give his evidence at court on many occasions. Most times, it was cancelled at the last moment, usually owing to legal arguments forcing the hasty revision of calling witnesses to give live evidence. Sometimes, he would receive notice of cancellation before leaving home but sometimes, he would be sitting in an airport waiting to board his Belfast flight. Eventually, he boarded to land at Belfast airport in the knowledge there was a full security plan in place to afford him protection. He travelled on another alias using a new covert identity and passport. On the aircraft touching down, he made sure he was the last passenger to deplane and that was the cue for two armed PSNI officers to escort him into a back room in their Special Branch office.

Next, a people carrier type vehicle with blacked out windows was used to drive him to a police station that looked more a prison than cop shop. There were high barbed wire fences, concrete chicanes and blast walls. Though Robbie had served in the military, he had never set foot on Northern Irish soil, so he considered the sights of fortified police buildings as a novel experience. Inside the safety of the police yard, he would change vehicles again – more blacked out windows – to set off for the hotel. At the hotel, he was handed over to one of the regular Cover Officers from the London office who told him the arrangements for his attendance at court. Robbie would be met by an armed PNSI officer who would escort him to Belfast Crown Court and sit beside him in the court room as his protector and bodyguard.

A few things struck Robbie about his protector. The PSNI officer was quick to tell him how much he detested the changes to the uniforms since the RUC changed to the PSNI in 2001. He hated the removal of the old Royal Crown. The new PSNI badge still had a crown but not that associated with the British monarchy. Instead, it featured the St. Patrick's saltire, and six symbols representing different and shared traditions: the scales of justice (representing equality and justice), a crown (a traditional symbol of royalty but not the St Edward's Crown worn by or representing the British Sovereign), the harp (a traditional Irish symbol but not the Brian Boru harp used as an official emblem in the Republic), a torch (representing enlightenment and a new beginning), an olive branch (a peace symbol from Ancient Greece), and a shamrock (a traditional Irish symbol, used by St Patrick, patron saint of all Ireland, to explain the Christian Trinity). Robbie found this baffling but many steeped in the history of the province may conclude it is but one small piece of evidence illustrating the deeply ingrained sectarianism rooted within the minds of many people in Northern Ireland.

The bodyguard must have known that the man in the dock, though not yet convicted, was a Loyalist paramilitary terrorist who had been suspected at one time of murdering Rosemary Nelson and wanted to kill a Catholic a week. Yet, Robbie felt more in danger from him than Jimmy. In Robbie's mind's eye, it wasn't hard to imagine his bodyguard sitting in court beside him twiddling his gun round his finger like a cowboy in a western movie, pointing it at him and mouthing the word 'BANG! They did not exchange phone numbers on his departure from the province, especially in light of other incidents.

This PSNI officer was Robbie's regular escort and bodyguard. He took him to and from court every day during Robbie's stay in Belfast. On one of the trips, Robbie asked him to stop at a local Co-op store as they were passing by so Robbie could buy a bottle of wine to drink later that day. He kindly agreed and he pulled up outside the shop. This was outside of the security procedures agreed between London and the PSNI but Robbie had no intention of telling anyone about it. In vain, Robbie checked all the aisles and shelves for a decent bottle of vino. Frustrated, he asked the guy behind the till where it was kept, only to be informed that they didn't sell alcohol. On returning to the parked car, Robbie told him that they don't sell alcohol.

The PSNI man said, "Yeah, I know that. None of the wee shops do. It's not like on the mainland."

Robbie was speechless but thought, *Twat!* Undeterred, Robbie asked him to stop at a big Sainsburys store further up the road. You could cut the atmosphere. Once more, the officer parked with Robbie off on his quest again. Success this time, as he triumphantly carried two bottles of plonk in a bright orange Sainsburys carrier bag back to his waiting escort. The drive to the hotel was accompanied by a deafening silence. Without a word, Robbie got out of the car to walk into the hotel reception area where he was met by the London Cover Officer who, on spotting the bag, said, "Where did you get that from?"

Robbie, still peeved by the PSNI officer's antics said, "Fuck me, Sherlock, you're meant to be a detective, the country's finest, the clue is on the bag." Not wishing to offend, Robbie added it was from Sainsbury's, just in case he was still struggling with the big clue. He told him his bodyguard had stopped on the way back. He also informed the Cover Officer all about the Co-op fiasco.

By the time of the Belfast trial, about six years had passed since Robbie last saw Jim Fulton in the Plymouth pub the night before his arrest by the armed Devon and Cornwall police team. By prior arrangement and in the company of his new best friend the bodyguard, Robbie entered the Diplock court by way of the judge's chambers. Although Muriel Gibson was tried on the same indictment, only Fulton occupied the dock. There were two sets of counsel, one for the prosecution and the other representing Fulton. Mr Justice Hart was sitting in a chair high above all else. As soon as Robbie entered the courtroom Fulton had him in his direct line of sight. They locked eyes as Robbie walked towards the witness box. Jimmy had a half smile on his face. Fulton nodded slightly, his chin almost imperceptibly rocking towards his chest then back once more. Most people would not have noticed. Robbie looked back and raised his eyebrows once in a gesture of recognition. It was only then Robbie noticed what Jimmy was wearing. It was the black suit he had bought with the money given by Neil for Jimmy to wear for the fake Lowry scam. Robbie thought he looked like one of the Beatles dressed in a three-quarter length box jacket depicted on a Sixties album cover. With supreme self-control, Robbie kept his face straight.

Later, Robbie often wondered how Fulton felt at that moment when Robbie changed from just a name in the court papers to a living, breathing undercover cop whom Fulton had considered a mate. Mates who for such a long time drank, ate, laughed and schemed criminal plots together, only for him to discover Robbie had tricked him. Robbie was the last man standing after the con had been executed.

Another incident of note happened in Robbie's hotel in Belfast. The hotel was situated directly opposite the cemetery where George Best is buried, so on most days people would visit his grave to pay respects to a gifted footballer. One early evening Robbie was sitting in the hotel and became aware of a big fella sitting on the stool next to him. They struck up some small talk conversation with Robbie primed to trot out a creative cover story if needed.

Robbie, acting naturally, said, "What is it you do for a living, big fella?"

Big Fella said, "I'm a police officer."

"Fuck me, mate, that must be a bit hairy over here, a police officer. How dangerous is that… respect to you, big man."

Big Fella said, "It is, and it's more dangerous for me because I'm an undercover police officer. A UCO."

Robbie, keeping a poker face and not knowing if this man was crazy, said, "Wow! You must be so tough and brave to work undercover. I don't think I could do anything like that. One hundred and one percent total respect to you, big man. What sort of stuff do you do, can you talk about it?"

Big fella replied, "I drive HGVs. That's about all I'll say..." He left it there with those words hanging in the air.

Robbie wanted to say, but dare not, "You're joking me, who would have thought two undercover police officers who drive trucks, coming from different countries, would bump into each other at a hotel bar in Belfast."

Robbie later told a UCO colleague that what happened was something he might do in the right circumstances. He would do it for the devilment and respect for a brother UCO. Robbie did add, "The big fella could have been an extra layer of officer safety, a covert protection team detailed to cover us while in the hotel. That would be standard operating procedure (SOP) on such a high-profile case. Maybe the guy was giving me the nod, you know, like drop it into the conversation that he's got my back. But the mention of HGVs made me think of the surveillance team when we were in Weston-Super-Mare, the chase to Exeter and the following day when Dave and I cleaned ourselves after we were followed into the caff. If we had a ghost team looking out for us during the operation, it would make sense not to tell us in case we started to act differently in front of Jimmy." Nevertheless, he always thought that was spooky coincidence on what was to be his last day using the alias of Robbie.

# CHAPTER 33

## The Admissions

The full transcript of the handed down judgement of Mr Justice Hart may be found under the reference of R v Fulton and Another, Neutral Citation No. [2006] NICC 35, Delivered 7 December 2006, Hart J.[16]
In this and following chapters, we include abridged or reduced versions of that full judgement. Just like a chef in the kitchen, the term "reduction" refers to a technique that delivers an intense flavour. The excerpts are intended to give you a taste of the essence of

---

[16] https://www.judiciaryni.uk/judicial-decisions/2006-nicc-35

the gravity of the crimes in the case of *R v Fulton and Gibson.*

We have also used two different formats for those excerpts to differentiate those parts where the judge is 'speaking' and the transcripts of the covert recordings *per se.* Those transcripts are unredacted and appear in the same form as they did at the trial.

It doesn't take a great legal mind to know the admissions secretly recorded by the Operation George undercover officers and the probes were the key to securing convictions in the cases of William James Fulton and Muriel Gibson. Without the admissions, there was nothing left of the Crown's case. Mr Justice Hart, the trial judge, put that in legalistic terms: *'The prosecution case depends entirely upon the alleged admissions by the defendants whilst they were under police surveillance, and the inferences to be drawn from those admissions. So far as Fulton is concerned, during the second interview the relevant tapes were played to him. He did not respond, and the third interview was cut short to allow him to consult with Mr Ingram [a solicitor]. In the fourth and subsequent interviews, Fulton accepted that it was him talking. This has not been challenged, and so I am satisfied that he uttered the words attributed to him in the transcripts. It is noteworthy that, unlike Gibson, no suggestion was made to any of the undercover officers or transcribers that the transcripts were an inaccurate record of what Fulton said, although, as we shall see, there were issues about whether everything relevant to the issues in the case had been recorded. As I am satisfied that Fulton uttered the words said to him, for the sake of brevity I will henceforth simply refer to them as the "admissions."'*

Undercover police officers are exactly that. They are still police officers masquerading as someone and something else. When deployed they are still police officers and all the rules that apply to everyday officers still apply. So, in simple terms, if they were to ask a question of someone stopped in the street that goes to the heart of the investigation: a direct question (*R v Bryce*), they must under Code 'C' of PACE caution that person. A short and unsuccessful career as a UCO would follow in that scenario so they must avoid the direct question and instead ask an indirect question (*R v Christou and Wright 1992*).

The case law of *Bryce, and Christou and Wright* were always at the forefront of the UCOs' minds when with Jimmy. He would start to talk about an event in detail. In simple terms he was giving the UCOs the evidence from his own utterance to convict himself. The UCOs' questions would have to be indirect questions so as not to make the 'conversation' inadmissible and rule out at any future trial. Otherwise, his self-admissions would have been deemed as inadmissible under Code C of PACE and never would have seen the light of a courtroom. To avoid the trap of 'direct questions' but to keep the conversation going in a natural way the Plymouth team of UCOs would say things such as, "Fuck me, Jimmy," or make an acknowledging grunt or similar noise, and Jimmy would continue with his talking about his involvement in the murders, robberies, pipe bomb and gun attacks, and other offences. Before we turn to the details of the case against Fulton, here are some procedural points

OPERATION GEORGE · 371

involved when undercover officers must give evidence at trial. In general, in the courts of England and Wales, when an undercover officer enters the witness box and has sworn the oath or affirmed, they will address the judge to inform the court that they are a serving police officer in the United Kingdom and for the purpose of this operation they were known as John or Jane. They then ask for the leave of the court to give evidence in that name. They often inform the court that they are in possession of a police warrant card if the judge wishes to see it. The UCO will have that warrant card ready to produce in case it is asked for. It will be tucked away inside an envelope safe in John's pocket or Jane's handbag.

At Belfast Crown Court in front of Mr Justice Hart, the procedure was different in that the UCO would write his real name and home police force on a slip of paper then placed inside a small envelope. That note was passed to the court usher who in turn handed it to the judge. He would open the envelope, read the information, and peer over his spectacles at the officer standing in the witness box a few feet away. The slip was then replaced into the envelope, sealed and placed with the judge's papers on the bench.

The preliminaries now completed, it's time for the fun and games to commence. It has been said criminal trials are not a search for the truth. Instead, trials are about what can be proved through evidence, using the rules of evidence. One of the aspects of the trials of Fulton and Gibson is in some ways it ran counter to the perceived wisdom of the penultimate sentence. The admissions were either true or not.

So many parts of a criminal trial can be fairly described as the play within the play. The examination and cross examination of any single witness can be as dramatic as any chapter in a book or film scene. It sticks in the memory like this exchange between Fulton's counsel and Robbie at trial because in our view it can also be seen as the play within the play. Fulton's counsel posed this question to Robbie. "Did you ever ask a direct question about any offences when in the company of Mr Fulton?" Immediately with Code C in mind, Robbie said confidently, "No, my Lord," as he addressed the judge.

Inevitably, the barrister challenged Robbie's strong denial, affecting an air of incredulity, "No, officer?"

Robbie, knowing he was on solid ground replied, "No. Not once, my Lord."

The barrister shuffled through the bundle of papers in front of him and directed Robbie to a particular bundle and page number. Robbie was now looking at a bundle of exhibits including transcripts of the tape summaries. These were transcripts he had helped to prepare some six years previously. He quickly took in what was typed and recalled the gist of the actual conversation. It was about an episode Fulton had recounted when he and others had driven out to the countryside in his wife's car, intending to murder a Catholic.

With no sense of haste, counsel permitted Robbie to settle before saying, "You are now on that page, yes?" Robbie confirmed he was. "Very well. This conversation took place between you and Mr Fulton on 18th September 2000 during a journey where my client was driving, and you were the only other person in the vehicle. Is that correct?"

"It is, my Lord," Robbie said.

"I will read the part of Mr Fulton and you will read your part, your words. Is that clear?" Counsel said.

Robbie had played this 'he said, she said' scene on many occasions in Crown Courts up and down the mainland. Robbie cleared his throat with a couple of light coughs and replied, "Understood, sir."

"Very good. Please start with your words at the middle of the page."

"What's been the biggest fuck up you've had though?" Robbie said.

Fulton's counsel began to read Jimmy's words, "Oh for fuck's sake, Robbie. I'll tell you…" He continued until the end of Fulton's comments before looking at Robbie, saying, "Please look at those words of yours once more, officer. Those that prompted what Mr Fulton had to say."

Robbie knew what counsel was referring to but said, "You mean, 'What's been the biggest fuck up you've had though?'"

"Yes. That was a direct question, officer. Wouldn't you agree with that proposition?"

Robbie replied without pause, "No, sir. That was not a direct question. I asked your client, 'What's been the biggest fuck up you've had though.' He could have told me he'd once fallen off a ladder or something of that nature. He didn't. He chose to tell me about his attempt to murder a Catholic."

A silence fell on the courtroom. In this vacuum, Robbie sensed the defence barrister's eyes burning into the skin of his forehead like two laser beams. He also thought, *Yes, you can see the words 'I'm not a twat' etched into my skin.* The barrister moved on to a few more secondary questions that were answered with yes or no replies. Then suddenly with no warning or indication he said, "No further questions, my Lord," and sat down. The Judge confirmed that he had no further questions and turned to the Prosecuting Counsel who also confirmed he had no more questions.

Robbie then heard the words that every police officer longs to hear, "You are released, officer, thank you."

Robbie returned the respectful dismissal with four simple words, "Thank you, my Lord." Robbie glanced across the court room at Fulton, taking him in for the last time. There was no more raised half-smile on his face. No more nodding of the head. No more friendship. Just a look of betrayal. Robbie had knocked the last few nails into the lid of Jimmy's coffin. Jimmy was alone down the rabbit hole, in the dark with no friends around him anymore. Robbie turned his back on him and walked out of the courtroom, followed by his assigned bodyguard. Operation George had finally come to an end for Robbie. The longest trial in Northern Ireland's legal history.

## Alcohol and Drugs

Mr Justice Hart also had to apply his mind to a question he often posed to himself in the judgement handed down on 7 December 2006. At one point in that document running to over ninety thousand words, the judge stated:

'I have considered, amongst other things, whether there is any reason to believe that this is, or may be the case, in each evidential tape, and I excluded a number of tapes because the prosecution were unable to show that Fulton was not, or may not have been, affected by alcohol and/or drugs. So far as the remaining tapes that were admitted are concerned there is no evidence to suggest that Fulton was affected by drink or drugs in any of them, and therefore no reason to doubt their reliability on that score. Had there been such evidence no doubt defence counsel would have asked me to listen to the tapes, as was done in relation to several of the tapes relating to Gibson.

The undercover officers Neil, Robbie, Dave, Max and Gary were cross-examined on this topic and gave the following evidence:

On 16 March 2006 at pages 9 and 10 of his cross-examination Max described how Fulton smoked some cannabis when they were on the move together in a car, although Max could not say whether Fulton or himself was driving at the time. Max was not surprised by this, and did not remonstrate with him, saying that it was not take [sic] significant because "the vast majority of the public smoke cannabis nowadays". Robbie took the same view when Fulton told him that he had smoked cannabis whilst having a drink at Gibson's house.

That on one occasion Fulton smoked cannabis whilst he and Max were traveling together lends support to the suggestion that Fulton may have used cannabis on occasions when he was traveling in a car, although I consider it most unlikely that on the occasion Max described Fulton smoking cannabis in the car Fulton was driving at the time because of the obvious risk to Max from such conduct. Whatever risks Fulton may have been willing to run, I do not believe that Max would have allowed himself, and other road users, to be endangered. It would also go against the strict policy laid down by Neil to which Gary referred. I remain of the view that I expressed at page 9 of my ruling of 8 May 2006, namely "that Fulton was anxious to show that he was reliable and conscientious individual in order to retain the favour of the undercover officers who he believed were employing in their criminal enterprise." That is a factor which would have influenced Fulton against driving under the influence of drink or drugs whilst he was with a member of the firm. Whether Fulton was affected by cannabis on any other occasion when he made admissions is a separate issue. If he was smoking cannabis when undercover officers were present, or had been smoking beforehand, I am satisfied that would have been obvious to them because their previous experience as uniformed officers would have enabled them to recognize the signs of someone having taken drugs or alcohol. For an example see Dave's evidence on 28 March 2006 at pages 86 to 89 where he described various symptoms of drug or alcohol use. On those occasions where they were not present, the only people who can say whether Fulton was affected by drugs or alcohol are Fulton and those who are present. Only if something is said, or there is something about the way people spoke, or there is some other evidence which would alert listeners to the conversation to this possibility, could the recording throw light on whether he was affected by drugs or alcohol. Any listener is dependent upon the recording in order to determine whether or not Fulton was affected by alcohol or drugs at the time.'

Mr Berry cross-examined Gary, seemingly on the instructions of his client, Fulton, putting to him that on three occasions he had given cocaine to Fulton. Firstly, in a pouch after Gary had visited the toilet in a wine bar, secondly, in Neil's flat after Neil had gone to bed, and on the third occasion a few weeks later when he allegedly gave Fulton a small toiletry bag to keep for a few days, accompanied by an invitation to sample the cocaine it impliedly contained. We say "seemingly" as it appears these allegations were a smear tactic dreamed up by Fulton in a desperate attempt to discredit the UCOs and the admissibility of the secret recordings.

## Gibson Legal Issues

Just as in Fulton's case, the Crown's case against Muriel Gibson depended entirely on the admissions she made both to undercover officers and recorded on the hidden probe that recorded her conversations at her home. However, it seems as if her legal team explored more avenues than Fulton's team did in trying to have the admissions ruled inadmissible. At an early stage of police interviews, she claimed not to recognise her own voice on a tape that was played to her. Indeed, apart from one brief passage, it was never admitted by Gibson nor her legal team that she was present on any occasion [of the recordings], or that it was she who said the words attributed to her by the transcribers [of the recordings]. However, Mr Justice Hart in a ruling on the issue said:

'… I was entirely satisfied that, with the exception of one brief passage, Gibson had been correctly identified as the speaker in the passages attributed to her.'

He gave his reasons for reaching that conclusion and also added:

'For the avoidance of doubt I repeat that I am satisfied that she was the speaker on all the occasions attributed to her unless I say otherwise.'

Again, like in the case of Fulton the issues of alcohol, drugs and direct questions put by undercover officers were all matters her defence team used to persuade the trial judge some or all her admissions were inadmissible. Part of the defence case was she was a heavy consumer of illicit and prescription drugs on occasion and material was placed before the court to persuade the judge of the validity of the defence submissions. Medical evidence was also before the court which the defence submitted went to the issue of an "abnormality of mind." In layman's terms there was some medical evidence that could mean any admissions were unreliable and therefore ought to be excluded from evidence.

The defence also suggested that the officers transcribing the transcripts "have sought to deliberately remove references to alcohol." But the judge made it clear that:

'… each of these evidential tapes has been excluded from evidence and were there a jury hearing the case the jury would not be permitted to consider the contents of the excluded tapes, and, unless the tapes were excluded after the voir dire, would not be aware of the contents. I agree that is a correct statement of the law and I must therefore ignore the contents of the excluded tapes.'

The judge also considered that "a number of general submissions were advanced in the closing submissions on behalf of Gibson… that as the admissions were not made under caution, and in an informal setting... [so] she had no reason to appreciate the importance of the occasion and the imperative to be measured and accurate in responses to specific police questions."

The judge continued:

'It is difficult to overstate the importance of the obvious fact that none of the alleged admissions was made under caution. This is not a mere technical requirement in the system under PACE... At no stage during any of the recordings relied upon against Mrs Gibson did she have any reason to take care to avoid inaccuracy or exaggeration or to expect that anyone would place any reliance on anything she said. It is a common human characteristic, more marked in some than others, to embroider or even invent stories or inflate the importance of one's own role in a given situation. Casual dishonesty of this nature is inevitably more likely to occur in the kind of informal settings in which all the assertions relied on by the Prosecution were made by Mrs Gibson.'

The judge then went into further detail about:

'… the dangers associated with placing reliance on assertions made privately in relaxed circumstances are compounded where the individual in question…'

He then listed those dangers and concluded:

'All of these factors are present to a greater or lesser degree in Mrs Gibson's case. [the judge then turned to further defence submissions] There are a number of comments I make about these points. The first is that there was nothing improper in the undercover officers demonstrating enthusiasm or interest in the topic of Loyalist terrorism, provided that they did not circumvent the protections for suspects contained in PACE. Indeed, their usefulness would be severely limited if they did not display such enthusiasm and interest. The second is that, as will appear, many of the admissions were made when no undercover officers were present. Gibson's willingness to discuss terrorist crimes at length with her family, and friends such as Fulton, shows that she needed no encouragement to discuss such matters. Admissions made in those circumstances cannot be said to have been made because of her contact with undercover police officers. The third is that to characterise the contacts between her and the undercover police officers as amounting to offers to her "of a range of inducements" to make incriminating statements is unjustified. The use of the term "inducement" implies that an improper incentive has been offered to the accused, as a result of which she has made an unreliable confession.

Looking at the evidence as a whole I am satisfied beyond reasonable doubt that Gibson did not suffer from an abnormality of mind at the time covered by these *tapes*… That is not to say there may not have been occasions when she was affected by alcohol or a combination of alcohol and prescription drugs, and occasionally cannabis, which may on occasion render her admissions unreliable and where there is evidence suggesting that was or could have been the case, I will exclude the relevant tape… I do not accept that, as her instructions suggested, she was drinking heavily or misusing prescription drugs, or taking illicit drugs on a virtually daily basis throughout this period.'

The issue of direct questioning was the subject of written submissions by the defence who submitted "all of the taped conversations between the defendant and Sam and or Dave S amounted in effect to the functional equivalent of an interrogation and should be disregarded." The judge responded:

'To a considerable extent these submissions repeat points which I have already considered when ruling on the admissibility of the evidential tapes and I do not propose to rehearse again my reasons for holding that the evidential tapes which have not been excluded were not the functional equivalent of an interrogation... A point upon which considerable reliance is placed is that Gibson was no longer free to resile from admissions she had made in conversations that have been excluded, and indeed was liable to expand upon them. Even though the admissions may be separated by significant periods of time, it is impossible to say that the later (admissible) admissions would have been made even if the earlier (inadmissible) admissions had not. This is a factor that ought to weigh heavily with the Court in respect especially of admissions made to Dave S and Sam, who repeatedly breached the rule that direct questions were not permitted to such an extent that they were removed from the covert surveillance operation.'

Mr Justice Hart continued:

'As the defence concede the court is bound to exclude from its consideration the contents of other tapes that have already been ruled inadmissible. Where the admission was not prompted, then there is nothing to cause the defendant to choose to speak, even if she repeated or expanded upon admissions she had made on other occasions, usually weeks, if not months, before. In those circumstances I do not consider that what Gibson may have said in an excluded conversation can be said to "taint" a later admission. On the later occasion she was completely free to decide whether to talk or not, and the admissions appear to be entirely voluntary and spontaneous. To suggest that her decision to talk about criminal offences she had apparently committed could be regarded as "tainted" by what happened long before is, in my opinion, unsustainable. She, like Fulton, was quite prepared to boast about her terrorist activities to those she thought she could trust, such as her family and/or Fulton. Unfortunately for her, her loquaciousness betrayed her when she was speaking to people who were, unbeknown to her, undercover officers. I consider that there is no basis for regarding her admissions as unreliable on that ground.'

In his final written judgement, Mr Justice Hart returns to the question of alcohol and drugs in relation to every single admission or admissions that the Crown say is sufficient to convict Fulton and Gibson.

# CHAPTER 34

## Sentencing and Appeal

William James Fulton was sentenced to a total of twenty-eight years' imprisonment. Muriel Gibson received an eight-year custodial sentence.

On 26 January 2007, the BBC reported[17]:

'A leading member of the Loyalist Volunteer Force has been sentenced to 28 years for the murder of Portadown grandmother Elizabeth O'Neill.

William James Fulton, 38, of Queen's Walk, Portadown, was jailed for 48 terrorist offences

---

[17] http://news.bbc.co.uk/1/hi/northern_ireland/6302441.stm

including attempted murder of four police officers.

Mrs O'Neill, 59, died in an explosion at her home in the mainly loyalist Corcrain estate in Portadown in 1999.

Mr Justice Hart ordered Fulton to serve a minimum of 25 years. His lawyers had argued at Belfast Crown Court that he should not serve more than 20 years because that was the longest term other paramilitary prisoners served during the Troubles. He was also sentenced to 28 years for the attempted murder of four police officers during the Drumcree dispute in 1998.

His co-accused, Muriel Gibson, 57, with an address at Clos Trevithick in Cornwall, was sentenced to eight years for LVF membership and destroying evidence following the murder of Adrian Lamph in 1998.

Passing sentence on Fulton, the judge said: "His culpability for what happened is greater than anyone else involved in this episode and I propose to sentence him accordingly. This was a very grave crime with many aggravating features and I think the minimum period necessary to satisfy the requirements of retribution and deterrence before he can be considered for release is 25 years imprisonment."

After the trial, Mrs O'Neill's son Martin said although he was happy that justice had been done, those who made and threw the pipe bomb were still at large and should give themselves up. Mrs O'Neill died after picking up a bomb which had been thrown at her home where she had been watching television.'

## The Appeal of William James Fulton

The Belfast Telegraph reported the outcome of Fulton's appeal in the following terms[18]:

'A leading loyalist secretly recorded talking about the killing of a Co Armagh grandmother has lost his appeal against being jailed for his part in her murder…

Judges branded Jim Fulton a "ruthless and vicious individual" who talked about genocide as a way of wiping out Catholics.

Mrs O'Neill's killing was said to be fuelled by sectarianism because she was a Protestant in a mixed family.

Rejecting submissions that there was insufficient evidence of an intent to kill, Lord Justice Girvan told the Court of Appeal yesterday that Fulton's statement that he "made

---

[18] https://www.belfasttelegraph.co.uk/news/genocide-loyalist-loses-sectarian-murder-appeal-28482820.html

sure she was touched" related to the attack on the O'Neill house, his use of terrorist methods and furtherance of loyalist paramilitary activities. The judge said: "The clear picture that emerges from the entirety of the recorded conversations, including those recorded by probes, is of a ruthless and vicious individual devoid of human sympathy or empathy and steeped in deeply sectarian attitudes and bitterness who was prepared even to give expression to and countenance the desirability of genocide." Lord Justice Girvan referred to one recording where Fulton declared that Catholics had to be "wiped out".

According to the probe evidence he stated: "That's our belief, if it doesn't work out we're finished. We have to kill every Catholic and believe in it." With Fulton providing nothing to back up claims he was under the influence of drink or drugs at the time, the three-judge appeal panel declared themselves satisfied with the verdict.

Fulton, formerly of Queen's Walk, Portadown, shook his head in the dock as judgment was delivered…

His trial was the longest in Northern Ireland's legal history.'

Only Fulton appealed his convictions. On 19 June 2009, the Court of Appeal in Northern Ireland handed down its judgement after considering his appeal. He had been sentenced to a total of twenty-eight years' imprisonment with no prospect of any form of early release. The court made it clear after thanking counsel for their submissions that it was also indebted to the trial judge in saying, "We must also pay tribute to the careful and meticulous judgment of the trial judge which sets out his analysis of the evidence and the law and the findings of fact with commendable lucidity."

The court quashed the convictions on Counts 3, 4, 9 and 11 and allowed the appeal to that limited extent. It affirmed all the other convictions. The sentence of twenty-eight years' imprisonment was unaffected by the appeal court's decision.

We must add at this juncture, the quotation above about the trial judge illustrates one of the major benefits of the Diplock courts. The judge did set out both the facts and the law with superb forensic skills and precision. By doing so, it permits any interested outsider to see and understand the reasoning behind not only the guilty verdicts but also the not guilty. That is something that is impossible with a normal judge and jury trial because there is no way of knowing what influenced a jury in returning the verdicts. Unlike the United States, it is forbidden in law for a juror in the UK legal system to speak to anyone about what goes on inside the jury room. The result is that many practitioners and policemen alike are often baffled at jury verdicts.

# CHAPTER 35

## Unanswered Questions

Despite the sterling efforts of Colin Port and the entire Operation George team including not only the undercover officers, cover officers, but also the listeners, transcribers and every single person involved at any level whatsoever, some questions remain unanswered to this day.

### Who Killed Rosemary Nelson?

The public inquiry[19] concluded at page 465: 'There is no evidence of any act by or within any of the state agencies we have examined (the Royal Ulster Constabulary (RUC), the

---

[19] https://www.gov.uk/government/publications/the-rosemary-nelson-inquiry-report

Northern Ireland Office (NIO), the Army or the Security Service) which directly facilitated Rosemary Nelson's murder. But we cannot exclude the possibility of a rogue member or members of the RUC or the Army in some way assisting the murderers to target Rosemary Nelson.' In addition, the report said, 'We are sure that some members of the RUC publicly abused and assaulted Rosemary Nelson on the Garvaghy Road in Portadown in 1997, having the effect of legitimising her as a target… We believe that there was some leakage of intelligence which we believe found its way outside the RUC. Whether the intelligence was correct or not, the leakage increased the danger to Rosemary Nelson's life… We believe that some members of the RUC made abusive and/or threatening remarks about Rosemary Nelson to her clients. This became publicly known and would have had the subsequent effect of legitimising her as a target in the eyes of Loyalist terrorists.'

In a special report[20] in Glasgow's *Sunday Herald* dated 16 June 2002, that newspaper's then-Home Affairs Editor, Neil Mackay wrote:

'MARK Fulton, the loyalist godfather who killed himself in his prison cell last week, has been named as the killer of Northern Ireland defence lawyer Rosemary Nelson.

Fulton, known in loyalist circles as "Swinger", was discovered by prison warders in Maghaberry jail in County Antrim on Monday morning. Fulton was found in his bed with his belt knotted around his neck. It's believed he was depressed and suicidal over fears that rival loyalist inmates were targeting him for murder.

---

[20] https://web.archive.org/web/20150924202247/http://www.highbeam.com/doc/1P2-9989660.

Sources close to Colin Port[21] - the deputy chief constable of Norfolk Police who is heading the inquiry into the March 1999 murder of Nelson in a car bomb attack in her hometown of Lurgan - said Fulton, who was once the leader of the Loyalist Volunteer Force, was "without question" the man who masterminded her assassination.'

To some degree, that article based on anonymous sources and dated some nine years before the public inquiry report was published may have some credence in that the inquiry concluded at pages 341 and 342 that:

'We believe that neither the RHSB(S) [Regional Head of Special Branch South Region] nor the Detective Inspector from Lurgan [the local Special Branch DI] would have been willing to

---

[21] All efforts to contact Colin Port have been unsuccessful.

characterise what was going on as drug-related had they seen the notes that we have been able to examine. In the context of what was known about the RHD [Red Hand Defenders] and the Orange Volunteers, all the signs pointed to something altogether more sinister and we do not discount the possibility that what was missed was in fact the genesis of the plot to murder Rosemary Nelson.'

That excerpt is within the context of the inquiry examining the activities of the LVF and Mark 'Swinger' Fulton in the time immediately preceding the murder of Rosemary Nelson. Intelligence reports concluded Mark Fulton had met a Loyalist bomb-maker in Maghaberry prison on 27 February 1999 where Fulton was being held on remand on a charge of conspiracy to murder.

For those interested in a further account of the Rosemary Nelson murder, we recommend reading the related material on the website of The Pat Finucane Centre.[22]

## Who Pulled the Trigger?

Just who was the cowardly gunman who rode up to Adrian Lamph and shot him in the head at point blank range? The family of Mr Lamph still seek justice as can be seen from a recent article[23] in the *Belfast Telegraph*. In 2018, the newspaper reported, "The brother of a young Catholic man gunned down by the Loyalist Volunteer Force in Portadown 20 years ago this week has said his family's grief is still as raw as ever." The article continued, "His brother Niall Lamph said: 'We still have no justice for

---

[22] https://www.patfinucanecentre.org/
[23] https://www.belfasttelegraph.co.uk/news/northern-ireland/family-of-man-shot-dead-by-lvf-still-hoping-for-justice-20-years-after-brutal-killing-36824615.html

Adrian's murder. We can't remember the last time anyone from the police has been in touch. It is as if we have been forgotten.'"

You may think that on any analysis of the covert recordings in the Operation George saga Muriel Gibson clearly said it was Gary Fulton who pulled the trigger that fateful day. Here is a reminder of the relevant parts of the judgement handed down by Mr Justice Hart:

'I am satisfied that the murder of Adrian Lamph was a sectarian murder; that the gunman was the person seen on a mountain bike by Mr McCandless; that the gunman removed his clothing soon afterwards, and that it was burnt in the alleyway in an attempt to destroy all the clothing, and hence destroy evidence linking him to the crime.'

And later referring to a transcript from a probe at Gibson's Cornwall home, the judge summarised the passage as:

'When Gibson arrived Gary (ie Gary Fulton) had already stripped off his clothes and was naked because he had nothing to change into, so she told him to hide behind a gate.'

Other passages from covert recordings in the judgement relating to Adrian Lamph's murder include:

*'Gibson says that she was seen by John Smith and someone she refers to as "Wee Michael" when she went out to pick up the gun after the Lamph shooting and found Gary Fulton naked in the alleyway.*

*… The gunman rode the bike past Lamph, called to him and "shot him right between the eyes, took the whole head off".*

*… She ran up to "Ronnie and Jill's yard" and found the gunman naked. "And I go, what, what, what do you want me to do what have you done."*

*… The gunman then told her to take the gun, which she did and arranged for it to be hidden.*

*… She told Swinger that she had lent him, i.e. the gunman, the t-shirt. She described it as unique.*

*… When it is realised that because the t-shirt is so distinctive she destroys six photographs of men wearing it*

*… I am satisfied that the admissions are reliable. They were entirely unprompted by any undercover officer or agent of the State. Gibson chose to describe her exploits to her friend Vanessa.'*

Some interviews were deleted from the papers. In the remaining interviews Gibson made no

OPERATION GEORGE · 413

reply when questioned about the Lamph murder, save that in [in one tape] she said that she was sorry for the Lamph family and their loss.

Those excerpts make out a *prima facie* case it was Gary Fulton who shot and killed Adrian Lamph. That proposition is not evidence in a court of law nor is what Gibson said admissible as it is hearsay. Yet, suspects have been arrested and questioned on lesser information. Was Gary Fulton arrested and questioned in connection with this murder? That is what we asked of the PSNI in a Freedom of Information request. The PSNI replied it "could neither confirm nor deny" Fulton had been arrested and questioned about the Adran Lamph murder. They did confirm the case was still "open."

We do know he was convicted of serious crimes connected to Loyalist paramilitary activities as recently as 2013 when the *Belfast Telegraph* reported under the headline 'Jailed - gang who used Barbie typewriter and bullets to blackmail victims out of £15k.' The article[24] said:

*"Four men, including a notorious loyalist and a convicted killer, who used a Barbie typewriter in a £15,000 extortion plot have been jailed for a total 17 years.*

*At Belfast Crown Court Judge David McFarland handed three of the gang, Portadown loyalist Gary Fulton (40), Philip 'Bug' Blaney (48) and associate Mark Briggs five-year jail terms each, and Daniel Hamilton (31) a term of two years and eight months for the 'Red Hand Defenders' (RHD) [the group who claimed responsibility for the bomb that killed Rosemary Nelson] plot.*

*Fulton, from Gillespie Court in Comber and Portadown men Briggs and Blaney, neighbours*

---

[24] https://www.belfasttelegraph.co.uk/news/northern-ireland/jailed-gang-who-used-barbie-typewriter-and-bullets-to-blackmail-victims-out-of-15k-29285194.html

*on the Westland Road, had all pleaded guilty to two counts of blackmailing £15,000 from two victims known only as witnesses A and B on dates between 21 February and 24 March 2011...*

*Blaney had served a jail sentence for the manslaughter of grandmother Elizabeth O'Neill, who died in 1999 after picking up a blast bomb thrown into her home and Jim Fulton, a brother to Gary Fulton, is currently serving a life term after he was convicted of her murder.*

*A prosecuting lawyer told the court how the couple known only as Witness A and B had been targeted by two hand-delivered letters containing bullets at their home and business addresses demanding they pay £15,000 or face "action with extreme prejudice by the Red Hand Defenders".*

*Witness A agreed to pay up after receiving a number of further demands threatening that his house and business would be attacked, but he had also sought the help of police.*

*He described how the first set of threats were followed up by a petrol canister being placed in a lorry owned by Witness A and, during a mobile phone call the following day, he was asked how he liked his 'present' and warning him the next one would be 'ignited'.*

*The court heard that the gang had targeted the witnesses because, aside from their legitimate business interests, they had left themselves vulnerable to blackmail and prosecution owing to their cultivating a substantial cannabis farm, for which they had subsequently been convicted.*

*Judge David McFarland… said, "the gang had engaged in delivering letters with bullets and other threatening behaviour, describing how Briggs, Blaney and Fulton 'had been behind' the plot with Hamilton the 'conduit.'"*

Historical Enquiries Team (HET)

The Historical Enquiries Team was a unit of the Police Service of Northern Ireland set up in September 2005 to investigate the 3,269 unsolved murders committed during the Troubles, specifically between 1968 and 1998. It was wound up in September 2014, when the PSNI restructured following budget cuts. The former PSNI Chief Constable, Sir Hugh Orde, described this as a massive mistake.[25]
The team never got around to investigating the murder of Adrian Lamph but it did in the drive-

---

[25] https://www.belfasttelegraph.co.uk/news/northern-ireland/destruction-of-historical-enquiries-team-was-massive-mistake-says-ex-police-chief-orde-34386735.html

by shooting of James Patrick, known as 'Seamus,' Dillon. He died in Dungannon at the hands of the LVF on 27 December 1997 the same day Billy Wright was killed by INLA. The LVF stronghold of Portadown and largely nationalist Dungannon are a short driving distance apart especially if using the motorway. In 2005 Muriel Gibson was charged with possession of the murder weapon used in the drive-by shooting but later acquitted. She was charged based on four tapes covertly recorded by the Operation George team. One tape was excluded by the trial judge owing to its inadmissibility because the judge found she was inebriated at the time of the recording. Three others were excluded as they contained no details to support the case against her on that count. In them, she was heard talking about Dillon's murder. There are no references to these in the official judgement because of their inadmissibility.

Bentley[26] has had access to the HET report into the Dillon murder. It names Gibson as a suspect along with several other prominent LVF members. The prominent members at that time were Jimmy Fulton and his brother Mark 'Swinger' Fulton along with their cousin Gary Fulton.

The LVF hid under the cloak of being called a paramilitary organisation. In fact, it was a firm: an organised crime gang specialising in murder, genocide, punishment shootings, drug dealing, extortion rackets, kidnapping, and robberies.

The Plymouth firm headed by Neil brought two[27] of them to justice.

---

[26] Bentley was the author responsible for all research connected to this book.
[27] Mark Fulton was arrested on 3 December 2001 and on the basis of evidence gathered by Operation George he was charged with the offence of conspiracy to murder. He was remanded in custody and committed suicide in Maghaberry prison on 10 June 2002: Para 31.134 Rosemary Nelson Inquiry Report. Gary Fulton was never arrested in connection with Operation George.

# ABOUT THE AUTHORS

Mark Dickens

Mark Dickens is a pseudonym. From humble, and sometimes, difficult beginnings in life, Mark served for many years in a British police force with distinction. He was commended on many occasions for his outstanding detective work including many undercover roles involving the infiltration of organised crime groups throughout the U.K. Mark was registered on the national undercover officer index and also ran training courses for undercover officers. Following his retirement, he remains anonymous to protect the safety of himself and his family.

Stephen Bentley

Stephen Bentley is a former British police Detective Sergeant, pioneering Operation Julie undercover detective, and barrister. He now writes in the true crime and crime fiction genres and contributes occasionally to Huffington Post UK on undercover policing, and mental health issues.

Stephen is a member of the UK's Society of Authors and the Crime Writers' Association. His website may be found at [https://www.stephenbentley.info/](https://www.stephenbentley.info/) where you may subscribe to his newsletter. You may also find him on Twitter as @StephenBentley8.

His Operation Julie memoir is also available in large print with the ISBN 978-6219619042.

## ACKNOWLEDGEMENT

The excerpts from the court judgement and the Rosemary Nelson Report are Crown copyright material and are covered by the Open Government Licence permitting reproduction in this book.

www.ingramcontent.com/pod-product-compliance
Lightning Source LLC
Chambersburg PA
CBHW081404080526
44589CB00016B/2475